PRAISE FOR ANTON JONES

Haunting, harrowing, darkly funny, heart-rending, compassionate, luminous, lustral—this is powerful writing! There are no half-measures here. I was hooked from the first few lines. Anton Jones has a keenly observant eye, an attuned mind, and a musical ear. He grabs the reader and takes them on a journey through the dark reaches of the abyss to the radiance and wakefulness of the light.

— MAURICE BOYER, D.M.A, PROFESSOR OF MUSIC, CONCORDIA UNIVERSITY CHICAGO

Jones educates, engages, and encourages reflection and connection with a color wheel of depth, contrast, and connection. Through a candid tour of their unique perception and valuable perspective, *This is Not a Death Sentence* is relatable and enlightening through creativity and transparency. Anton Jones shares an engaging memoir that is written elegantly and with precision.

— DR. ANDREA DINARO, CHAIR, DIVISION OF CURRICULUM, TECHNOLOGY, AND INCLUSIVE EDUCATION, CONCORDIA UNIVERSITY CHICAGO

A bold and powerful way to tell a personal story! Anton is so deliberate with his word choice and each poem's unique formatting that it's almost like sleight of hand the way he draws you into his world, enabling readers to take this engrossing trip through his past with him.

— MIKE CURTIS AUTHOR OF *AROUND THE WORLD IN 80 SANDWICHES*

Jones's writing abrasively bridges the gap between reality, delusion, and the human struggle in only a way that poetry can, leaving the reader questioning what is real, what is good, and how it is that humanity can preserve in the face of its own inadequacies. Jones opens the door of mental illness wide and, in deftly exposing his reality, provides gut-wrenching truths, painful struggles, and even a glimmer of hope.

— JOSIAH HAHN, EDUCATOR

Readers are in for a powerful depiction of a journey navigating mental illness that is sure to stick with them beyond the final pages.

— ERIC BAKER, SONGWRITER, WRONGBIRD

This is Not a Death Sentence

a Memoir in Verse

Anton Jones

This is Not a Death Sentence

a Memoir in Verse

Anton Jones

EMPOWERED PRESS

Published in the United States by The Empowered Press, LLC, Florida

ISBN 978-1-957430-24-9 (paperback)

ISBN 978-1-957430-25-6 (ebook)

Library of Congress Cataloging Publication Data is available.

http://theempoweredpress.com

publish@theempoweredpress.com

Cover Design: Onur Aksoy

http://onegraphica.com

Layout Design: Katie Moody

For my family.

CONTENTS

Author's Note xi

PART I
THE MIDWEST

1. Hemisphere 3
2. Eternal Recurrence I 5
3. The Heart Describes the Body to its Captor 7
4. Laniakea 10
5. Waiting for Mail 14
6. When There's Nothing to Stand On 16
7. Warning Signs 17
8. I Went Walking 20
9. Responsibility 29
10. Collision 30
11. Apotheosis 32
12. My Father Was a Carpenter 36

PART II
PORTLAND

13. Door to Door 41
14. The Bog 42
15. Apoptosis 44
16. The Custodian 47
17. Life Is Made Possible by the Lies We Tell Ourselves 48
18. Duane Street, Oregon City 52
19. Ghosts of Times 54
20. Sleeping/Body Bag 56
21. Corneal Ulcers 58
22. Mt. St. Helens 60
23. Everything is Fine 62
24. Saturn Devouring His Son 63
25. Bullous Myringitis 64
26. Getting Out of the House 67
27. Drip 68
28. Everything Is Fine II 69

29. Like Needles 71
30. Atmospheric Entry 74

PART III
THE TRUTH WAS MEANT TO SET YOU FREE

31. And if That Is What Breaks You 77
32. Unravel 88
33. Lyric 104
34. The Custodian II 106
35. Last One to Die: Please Turn Out the Lights 107
36. Break the Rules 108
37. Antagonize 110
38. Haunt 111
39. Walking Away 112

PART IV
ALL THE THINGS I THOUGHT I WOULD NEVER SEE AGAIN

40. The Custodian III 121
41. The Voyage (to Epitaph) 123
42. Unused Wedding Vow 132
43. The Eulogy 134
44. Daily Work 137
45. Adobe Deli 141
46. Thanksgiving for the POMC 143
47. Counterpunch 148
48. Eternal Recurrence II 149
49. Love in the Ring 150
50. This Is Not a Good Poem 152
51. You Cannot Look Away 155

Acknowledgments 157
About the Author 159

AUTHOR'S NOTE

During my first year of high school, I didn't know I needed to be medicated. I didn't know about my family history or the spiders lurking in my genetics. As far as I was concerned, I was completely indestructible.

I thought I was reasonably normal, maybe a bit socially naïve (which, along with my exaggerated running form, earned me the nickname "Forrest Gump") but there was nothing considerably wrong. If anything, I was excelling in sports and classes.

During my sophomore year of high school, I woke up one morning and there was an anthropomorphic shadow leaning against my wall. He sauntered over, kneeled on top of my chest, and punched my sternum repeatedly until I gained enough control to punch back. I tried to rationalize this as a sleep paralysis nightmare. When it kept appearing long after I woke up, I thought I was being possessed. I woke up one morning from a dream that would continue regardless of if I was asleep.

I should be upfront. This is poetry disguised as a memoir, or maybe it's the other way around. I was having auditory hallucinations in eighth grade. It was mostly scrambled eggs: static in quiet environments, subconscious babble, intrusive thoughts, loosely associated and disorganized internal monologues. But I didn't know this wasn't normal—at least, not until I started hearing voices that seemed supernatural.

By the midpoint of high school, I was hearing what I thought was the voice of God and waging spiritual warfare against shadows. I was being bombarded by hallucinatory voices of ghosts telling me to do unspeakable things. That is, if I could understand what they were saying at all. Sometimes it's scarier when you can't make sense of the noise. There were so many more negative, intrusive thoughts and auditory hallucinations, that I was desperate to believe the one that seemed the most logical to me at the time: "run, Forrest, run." And I did. I ran away. I left my house barefoot and walked seven miles to church because I thought I was about to be possessed by a legion of sternum-punching demons.

As a result of being a minor, they insisted on not giving me a diagnosis, but they did medicate me with risperidone for the hallucinations. I took it until I went off to college. I did my best to hide symptoms as I was instructed to. If I wanted to retain some sense of normalcy, if I didn't want to be stigmatized before people even knew me, I had to keep it a secret. About a handful of people knew, and even less of them knew the full extent. Since I pride myself on working hard and adapting, I did well at pretending that everything was fine.

Though I wanted to speak, my internal voice was so often drowned out, leaving me paralyzed to do anything other than run in place. I was being held captive in my head by something I couldn't name.

PART I

THE MIDWEST

The tarp pulled across
Over my cousin's pool
Nobody's fooled by artificial blue
With crinkles like veins
Summer in a body bag

Hemisphere

Is
this—
no, this
is how
poems break:
an apoptosis of
syntax. I syntax for
light, and language breaks
cacophony into numerous sullen
bells and chimes. We are all chimes
and chiming misdirects and flavor tones
and I—I knocked over a vase of flowers at the
funeral service. The carpet gurgled and punched
floorboards; petals drifting down, never finding tilled ground.
I'm sideways with the curvature of the earth because booze spins
too fast. Apoptosis: a guest at a ball of victims—no, they didn't victim,
they hit the ground a little faster than me. I am no more than bones
scraping across sandpaper, but I am tired of this lineation, so I'll try

prose. We are here to bury my cousin and contemplate what's next. Imagine with me the above white space where earth is intangible, these words—your stars, and for once, we are allowed to grasp them without light speed. It's an old violence: memory and its consequence—that you would have to pay so much just to remember pleasant things, like flooring a golf cart through a cornfield. Love haunts just as much as any ghost. It drives hiccups down paths of pain left in the reserved seats of the front-row pews; fog wracked by the pursuits of wonder, wonderful pain, and what resurrection looks like in reverse. But I wasn't sure about what's next, ascension or extinction, so I tipped over a candle too and the flame still points up. Nothing sideways about it. Fire eats the dead tissue, energy trapped in things once alive. In this moment, this is my confirmation that my cousin is with God. But that doesn't mean I'm not upset. I gave the eulogy and the words bounced off stained glass. They are striving ceaselessly still to find a place of their own. The action of eulogy is the hemisphere made for me. I play hopscotch across its freshly drawn, soon-gone horizon, the imaginary haunt between earth and stars, grounded and abstract, the living and the not. It's hard to say dead, but let the final words these dead ears hear be ones constantly approaching the asymptote of ineffable. Let this vision improve with the lens of our welling tears. Let them destroy us in their very utterance, for once spoken, it is unmaking.

Eternal Recurrence I

I imagine myself small and sticky
from eating a sucker but sucking
quietly as the ceremony was carried out
with no pallbearers, no box
of fine and shiny wood.
What happens to these people
when we can't find their bodies?

It is natural to think of the lies
and what lies after
the casket is lowered—
but when there is no body to bury,
when the forest swallows someone
without ceremony, I found
my tiny self thinking
that without the burial, the closure
of the casket, the spirit
lies in the eternal recurrence
reliving the moments that caused their death
over and over, since they never found rest
under a dirt mound and polished stone.

Though I imagined the fatal actions
were played out on repeat,
I can't help but think the emotions and thoughts
were left up to the choice of the spirit—
though you must continually experience your death
you are free to think of it whatever you please.
It is a purgatory.
So, in the event that I die and my body
is never recovered
I feel the need to prepare myself,
to select the emotions I will choose to feel.

Say, if death finds me captive in a stranger's basement,
hands bound and the only sight greeting me
are the matrices of fragmented light
phasing through the burlap sack over my head,
and I have to live my ever-moment
slowly, as the knife cuts
or in flashes like bursting lightbulbs
as the wooden bat makes contact with my ribs,
I will have been prepared, so no,
it will not be fear
but the grateful contemplation of the objects
presented to me, the roughness in the touch to burlap
there is nothing like it and how it is
the executed's new face
but for children
it is a means of transportation
praised for its ability to restrict movement,
a vehicle for laughter as they hop around and fall.
I will think of the history of the stainless steel knife
and how many other types of blood it has tasted
yet cannot remember, as it was engineered
not to memorize with its body
because the past is a weakness:
the signs of chips, warps, and, yes,
even rust from unwashed blood
and blood's notorious ability to stain.
As my ribs break, I will think of how both
the bat and my bones were designed to flex
with impact, how both were made of dense interlocking
living fibers, and that it is possible the tree,
when the saw gnawed on its torso,
cried out louder than I did, with an ineffable
tongue all its own. A creaking
while my ribs respond with cracking
so now in death, I can talk to trees.

The Heart Describes the Body to its Captor

For me, the heart, it was
always the smallest
acts of kindness
that kept me
up at night.
That I once fell
for a girl, Laniakea,
because she came up behind me
and without a word
tucked in my obstinate
shirt tag. Being the heart,
it's hard to explain
affection like that
to the bicep.

Speaking of bicep, my eighth-grade coach,
Mr. Jensen, would ask for
another rep if he wasn't quite satisfied with our performance
citing to do "one more for the Gipper."
The smart-ass fifteen inches below me told him
to know the origin of the phrase
before digging it out of the crypt.
He presented to me a fully researched paper
when I graduated eighth grade
telling the story of how a coach
would try
to win
a game
against
an undefeated team
in the name
of a dying athlete.

I am grateful to coaches.
They help develop the rest of the body.
Our femurs, for example, I've been told,
can support 6,000 lbs before
they snap. One day I will
beat strong enough too.

I write this not to the bicep or the ass or the femurs,
but to the twitchy one, the brain,
who seems to require the most of me.
Though he has all of the body
under very strict rule
I am the one who most rebels—
placed in solitary
in the basement
because I'm known
to incite others to my cause if I have the voice.

We name him after his symptoms:
Affectless, Paranoid, Disorganized, Catatonic,
though I still have hope
I can make him feel more despite it.
I just need the right memory.
I taught myself to speak his language
but this is not how
I prefer to communicate
like this:
the eyes inform me that they are watching
one of my friends and his two brothers
sing "I Will Rise"
at the funeral service
for their own father
who I knew
as Coach Jensen,
who died of a heart attack.

I incited the eyes to weep.
Even the femurs felt weak.

A heart attack.
Of course the brain would blame me.
It makes me look so violent.
In reality, what they describe as a heart attack
is more of a resignation without notice,
effective immediately,
usually because of the trauma
the brain expects us to endure.
We get tired sometimes, we can't
stop beating, we
can't sleep.
A true heart
attack is when I, for the briefest of moments,
convince the rest of the body to dance with her
even though the brain had forbid it. A heart
attack is when I take over,
not when I stop working.

When Laniakea told us to never change,
she didn't poke the head.
She pressed her finger against me.

Laniakea

Though this is a delusion,
I know your fingerprints
and how they recount your past
since they are not far off from other identities and timekeepers of nature,
like tree rings—a unique complexity shared.
And all these patterns help me pinpoint time,
dog-ear specific moments, like when I ran
my hand through your hair last night.
It streaked—your hair and the night—and shimmered
like a waterspout offsetting our momentarily
untangled lives. Your hair,
caught in my fingers: filaments. They all sprout
from your skin and wait for our lives
to be combed apart again. But I
want the intersect. I like seeing
your bedhead before the sun's behest of light
and the night's bonfire smoke still caught in your hair.

You fell asleep again,
this time on my couch.
Though you still refuse to tell me
your real name, I have to call you
something. So, you will be Laniakea,
because your cardigan reminds me—
an image of space I once saw.
Your clothing, and probably space too, a hand-me-down
evident from fibers fraying out and shocking the beams
of quiet light with the reflective tendrils of autumn.
These filaments woven together,
like chlorophyll-tattooed leaves
for an hour of color, all of which
are caught in my retinas. Your image
reversed, flipped along the synapses—clusters

of gray matter syncopated with my anticipated
future lives. The mechanics of calculated
moment: your next words and what to say
at the lungs' breath out. It's all a bronchiole flexing web
which becomes vibrations and then voice
through the current instant following pathways
          of nitrogen,
                    oxygen,
                              carbon dioxide and
the air soup that found itself in my room.

And you laugh, think I'm absurd, when I tell you
that your voice is violin strings
since it reminds you that the strings
are made of fine strands ripped from sheep guts.

               What an experience of music!

And I remind you,
the bows that slide against the strings
are hair too, more filaments. Guts against hair jostle,
friction makes frequency. Somehow, in this expanse
we found a way for dead cells to make music.

Though this is
a delusion, it is
the most alive I have ever felt.

I lead you outside through your protests. You think
you need to scrape the bristles against your teeth; need
the teeth of a comb to untangle your hair.
I smile and say, "Sometimes, you barely need your shoes."
Sometimes you need to see filaments
to firmament, like the lens of
God sitting on bespeckled wet grass—words we can see

exchanged in the chilled air soup as we sit outside
looking into the forest. Everything still dripping
from the prior night's storm. It put out our bonfire.
And of course, we stayed outside anyway.
It was a rain that somehow felt warmer
than the fire, and I'm guessing you
might have had something to do with that.

You say your astigmatism
scatters the sun's light into looped strings.
You tell me your bad eyes can see
the sun's magnetic field and all it touches:
            your cheek,
                        my arms,
                                    this puddle at our feet
which is casting, like our eye, an upside-down flipped image
of Sol and even further beyond: strands of light
tangled in an illusory massive complex—Laniakea—
the structure of this present that ticks against entropy
before the cosmos goes dark.

And if this is just a delusion—
what could be
in reality—I am
a basement in the heart.
Though I am rushing to the end,
and the expansion will eventually
pull us apart, at least, in the visible now, we are:
            Laniakea—
                        Immeasurable Heaven—
                                    your lips against mine.

In 2014, the region of space that houses our galaxy and one hundred thousand others was given the name Laniakea. However, recent studies have shown that none of the superclusters that make up Laniakea are gravitationally bound. They just temporarily appear to be. It is a delusion. Dark energy will eventually disintegrate the body of Laniakea, each former fragment alone in its own pocket of darkness until it gets cold enough to vanish, until it will be hard to tell a supercluster that massive ever existed at all. Sometimes, if you tell a love story in reverse, you arrive at the ending you were always looking for.

Waiting for Mail

Though I haven't seen you in two years
I followed the instructions
to the letter
and sent one to you.
The word "waiting"
seems to necessitate
a "what" that is being waited for.
But there's no promise
that "what" will ever arrive.

What is in
the letter?
Voter registration.
"What" is in
the letter.
As in, I don't know
what
I am voting for.
It doesn't seem
human. No longer
a "who" but a "what."

What is in the letter?
Credit card offers.
I'm not in this letter.
As in,
this is not addressed
to me. But to
"whom" with the promise of
dollar signs and yet longer
APR droughts for
at least
twelve months.

What is in
a letter
if but a piece of me
from that moment
hoping it reaches
a piece of you
far from now.
It is not instantaneous.
There is a chance
that you
have grown
from the sending
to the receiving—
an understanding
I could not
have predicted.
And chance
it gets lost
or I get the address wrong
or you just stubbornly don't check your mail.
Even so, I still hope
that I am communicating with someone
at the dead letter office
whose face is warmed by message embers
whose hands are coiled in paper cuts
who appreciates the idea of us together
if the reality is not a must.

When There's Nothing to Stand On

Sometimes I imagine my skin
Is made of floorboards
I imagine that there is sheen
And polish and hardness
Covered in grain and tree rings
A subtle texture between the pores
And numerous trees have been hacked up
And patched together
To make me
The rot that's concealed underneath
That black mold creeping through the cracks
What was left of the organic material
Fed to a fungus

Warning Signs

It was in eighth grade that I became drawn to mathematics and symbols.

I had always been a meaning-maker.

A teller of stories.

A liar.

I was writing down stories about the math when I started experiencing what I called auditory intrusions and scenic interruptions—breaks and tangents in conscious thought, scrambling of the mind, hallucinations. It made me quieter in school because I was always listening for something no one else could hear.

I started having problems sleeping. My body just wouldn't let me. I would stare at the ceiling for hours and maybe get about three hours of shut eye. But I never felt tired.

I convinced myself I was superhuman. Everything around me contributed to this delusion.

My senior year of college, I was all at once an RA, a writing center consultant, a tutor for classes I had not taken, a factory worker, track athlete team captain, ultimate frisbee player, InterVarsity student leader, business manager of our literary magazine, student assistant to the Department of Philosophy and Religion, Phi Kappa Tau chaplain, and church work volunteer. I was teaching myself to play the didgeridoo, writing two 100-page novellas, taking an overload of classes, hiding symptoms, and refusing student loans, instead preferring to work off my debt. This was my proof I was superhuman.

My friends paid me the compliments, which further convinced me still. They called me more of an unstoppable force of nature than a human being. Until I suddenly couldn't hold back the symptoms in Portland. Though still undiagnosed, I knew what was happening. But I enjoyed it. I enjoyed the manic states that seemingly made me indestructible and able to do so much more work than everyone else.

I was always trying to find the limit to how much I could carry. In an attempt to control the symptoms, I would release the restraints all at once when alone so that I could manage it more easily in front of others. These became periods of isolation delving into esoteric ecstasy. Honestly, I was very high on myself and my manic mind. I calculated my free time down to the minute with elaborate spreadsheets. I would find the patterns of movement, thought, events that would create a unified theory of everything, and write them all down. I rehearsed conversations based on these rhetorical calculations, I created my own language to mess with my friends, I structured my day to the mathematical revelations, I informed my goals to its alignment. There was a musical theory to the pattern of my steps and the path I took to each class that would influence and inform all good things for all good people. And I was the creator and controller of this metaphysical madness. This was the beauty in the math I convinced myself I could understand.

Years later, my mom would find some of the notebooks and spreadsheets I kept. It was completely undecipherable. Gibberish. Half of the words were written backwards. I was not superhuman, just a delusional try-hard becoming hyperbole.

I would break from reality several times in high school, but my family and I could hide it. I eventually learned how to detect the warning signs of the breaks, so that when I lived alone in college and occasionally break, no one would ever know. I would isolate until the episode was over and then continue about my business. As far as I could tell, none of my peers suspected anything was wrong, they just thought I was weird. And that was the greatest high—that I could manage periods of hallucinations, mood disorders, and delusions without anyone ever raising concerns—that was the ultimate proof of my superhuman nature. Everything in my external environment was proof of my success.

I was convinced that my irregular mind enabled me to be good at calculation, abstraction, association, intuition, and deciphering meaning. I was convinced that the internal suffering, the hallucinations, the mood disorders, the scattered brain, all that I was told to hide, was good. It was not.

I am a liar. I am a liar. I am a liar. And I got very good at lying to myself.

This art is not becoming of you

You are

Not

Becoming

Art

Art does

Not

Necessitate

The suffering of the artist

Even now as I write this, I am worried that people with similar struggles will get the wrong idea. If you create and think that your experience of suffering makes your art good, and maybe, subconsciously, you keep destroying yourself to make the art, then please know that it does not make your art better. It only limits the amount of art you will create over your shortened life span. If you think your suffering is needed for art, all you are doing is killing yourself in a display case and making your friends and family pay to watch. You hurt them perhaps more than you allow yourself to be hurt.

I Went Walking

I stubbed my toes on both coasts
tripping over Nebraska and landing at Monument Valley
for reeling the landscape in too fast
I liked to consume
I overlooked people like I did fruits of the soil
but this mirror less walked and more
dawdled
a backpack strung over each shoulder
as he stumbled and tripped on his feet and his slurs
he followed the shadow of me
that went the other way
what was said in having no home
in his cargo pants and boots
scraps of hair left
and eyes that couldn't come to rest
just parsley
and I shirked another street
just another version of me
another Cain who had bashed an Abel
and set out after God had cursed the nature he made
He called me once too
put a whisper in my head
and commanded
go walking
and I did
I walked to the other side
a ridge of pines
rose up to greet me and
I was no closer to God than before I walked
since the voice of God
was one of my first
auditory intrusions
it made me wonder

if the devil was also capable of miracles
had the time
the longing
to talk directly to me
I kept walking and found Seattle and needle
where more Cains sat beneath the shade of metal proximate
and cardboard intimate
injecting the Babel in their veins
and their future scared me to action
I felt more in danger of hell for watching than falling
mission work and forest fires, Cle Elum, WA
we went into that valley
like a comet
and the mountains
pressed up their hands
to catch the Earth's blue hide
goosebumps
jumped on my skin
as holy music blasted away
the scenery I saw
with imaginary eyes
and I felt noble without having done anything right
transcendent
with feet firmly planted on the land
but the saddest thing was
I tried
to recreate those moments
painting a fence
setting a deck
rebuilding communities after disasters
but the moments eluded me every time
I wanted evidence
that my memories
were real
and I can't tell if failing to recreate them

meant that
they were
at my first funeral
they asked me to write the eulogy
and be the last goodbye
I complied and breathed the distance
that separates the beloved and the casket
with my frail
shaking voice
a voice that only wanted to go back
to childhood and Applebee's in Punta Gorda
where I could revisit the places he touched
I walked his new home on my left shoulder
out of a church with five others
my grandpa on my mom's side who seemed to always walk
in the right direction
even with Lewy Body Dementia
he was always so kind
and death does not deserve him

*

my cousin died before I could
when I walked in front of him in Chicago
he lagged behind when I tried
to press the pace
for the departing train we almost missed
he got on another train
I know why he was walking slow
and I couldn't see it until
I walked again in that city
where everyone walks so fast
and crawls so slow
and cries so fast
and heals so slow

so
is it a sin to blame God
when He unmakes His own creation
a grandpa and a cousin
left their shoes by the door and went walking elsewhere
for what reason should we be strong
when being strong
strong
strong
strong means you can't
break
and we did
we played football after we buried
a senior in high school
to show we could
break
be more than our tears

**

but here I am
and there you are
I can't write about walking
without walking over her
and is it a sin
to blame God for making her
the reason
I think
I lost my soul
or was my devil already there
I was an owl watching her night
as the walls went up
hands closed
Laniakea would have let the world use her as a dish rag

to wash its feet
but even the world knew better
most of the time
mine were dirty
she made me feel like steel wool
and terrified
and ecstatic
and feeble
and boundless
and I was living out of my mind
it was pathetic
really
I would make sure I walked
down the hallway at a precise time
hoping she would be passing
and throw me a smile
but if my memories serve me correctly
I romanticized the hell out of it
if I can't spite myself
I don't trust anyone else to do it
as often as I need to anyway
God knows Laniakea never did
and is it a sin
if I started to call her
Gretchen instead
giving me
a more accurate name
someone better stare at the ceiling for me
I was trying not to fall asleep with her on my mind
it was dangerous

and her friend
and my teammate
committed suicide

which mangled her entirely
almost in her sleep
her hair changed color
and her eyes found interest in the ground
averting any hand that came her way
I wanted to save
simple
if I was an honest man
but I am a liar
all the same
I went walking

***

after his suicide
I took idealism as penance
just holding onto what's left
before it got out of hand
which it already was
even before I chucked it
and I wrote her letters
from a basement in my heart
and I'll swear until I die
the basement was still a part of my heart
and not a part of something else
I sent her a letter when I was in
Michigan
Ohio
Maryland
Iowa
please hear me when I say
though a devil carried me around the country
I was never distracted from you
even when I tried to be

year after year
the letters told a little bit more
of what I was
hiding to say
feel this hand
it wants to heal your heart
but I squeezed it instead
and didn't even have the courtesy to clean up the mess

****

a man who would court her
stopped suddenly and said
that Gretchen was tainted meat
that she was mad with grief
and I howled inside
how dare he use
that name
revealed

"that though [I] never intended to sell [my] soul for evil
[I] would have damned [myself] without the help of a devil"

I wanted so badly to scrape the tissue out of that man's neck
to savage his face
because I'm an animal again
because I refuse to let any more lambs be sacrificed
because even in hindsight
I pray that God would let me tread there again as Cain
because I'm hungry
and I'm able
and on principle
I should claw and chew and grind and swallow
and

and

I got my dance
when Gretchen answered my letter
after it got lost in the mail
she found me two days before
and I couldn't look her in the eyes
because she was finally alive inside
and I did my worst to kill it again
I am imagined tears
I left
her in the cold
too ashamed to ask for an answer
too scared of the self I was becoming and
I went to spend my nights alone
I went to walk these years alone
unlike her
walking never went walking with me

*****

there are no antagonists here
only time
the devils are the ones I hallucinate
and I, an animal again,
I walked out with a whimper
though it was the loudest noise that I could make
there's been a boot on my throat for so long

******

I know there is a place
where my feet have raptured shadows
where mist coils around passing limbs
clinging to some

ancient conquering spirit
who had his face set on
what the destination meant
and not the walk
where every person is an asterisk
and every asterisk is a step in the wrong direction
without even
dementia
as an excuse
I hope to learn from
I hope this examination forces me to gurgle and rinse
so my feet don't step through
the black mold floor
I will take excursions through crypts
and swallow droughts in my stride
that Jones Pace
restlessness incarnate
I have a neck that defies compunction
so when I hear the foreman digging my grave
I will stride on even still
and I will build
furniture out of cinder blocks
useless though they be
stack sandstone mesas
create a Monument Valley for Mephisto
out of the places I walked
and the voices I hallucinated
to and toward
through and over
and always away

****

Responsibility

My mom was concerned with my tendency to isolate. When I was a junior in high school, we got into an argument. She wanted to spend more time with me, and I said I had the right to be alone. I will not accept help that I feel is unearned. I will not save myself until I feel worthy. But I did see what it did to her. I saw helplessness, and I believed I could save her from a monster of my own making. It is irresponsible for me to blame my illness for the hurt it causes others. I finally told her what I had been seeing and hearing: dozens of distinct visual and auditory phantoms telling me to kill myself and worse. I had never told anyone. Though it is irresponsible, there are reasons for wanting to be alone. I was then medicated for the hallucinations for a time, but the suicidal ideology wouldn't stop—which of course, I lied about. The most frequent fantasy was letting go of the steering wheel and relinquishing the control I had always strived so hard to gain.

Collision

Bring steadfastness
this last drive:
dust stings my skin,   pores,   invades my nostrils, fire breath
from Fireball—
the kind that singes foundation, rocks the balance, the kind
that bursts the fragmenting mind
into shrapnel,
sticking hot steel debris into my loved ones' faces   cutting
easier than carpet
slapped down
to cover up
wild froth,   the dried bloodied crust at the corners of my mouth
—it's my head
eating my teeth,
the burning gifts for the coroner   smell of burning rubber.
The eyes,

the world reflecting
forward   glances back
in the rear-view mirror
the parabolas
between my ribs
these bones that ring
when they aren't soul—
the coda that ladles syrup
on my cerebellum   everything is slow
and their eyes make me cower. My skin
rots off my carcass in the headlights and exposes
the hollow.   What is expression
without face? It's all cut up and my teeth are gone.
I can't breathe, speak, and the screams are not
my own.
Petrification   and the silicate sing

tightening the joints, freeze frame, hold
still   I will be this forever. Missed the brakes.
I once promised I would never change.
Here's my chance
to monument
to statue, on my way to the mausoleum, a sidewalk cross,
solidify, print my snow angel in cement,
I want a cement cocktail—submerging my DNA into mason jars filled
with gasoline from a puncture hole in a gas tank, oil
well, oil
spill
down   my
neck and those hairs can still stand on end   though coated in sludge,
muck, mustard gas,
gas tank has a puncture hole. I'm up
side down. Glass
all over the road.

The ones in blue, white, red   tread on.   There are sirens: the
wailing
echo of the night pitch
perfect, freeze
frame. "Hold still. We're coming to getcha." But whatever's left of me
isn't coming out.

Apotheosis

I.

Since you are delusional
you don't want to be human.
You want to be *The David.* *but you're a leper.*
You want the Psalmist to write your hymns. *but you're damned.*
So be more—and this is
the beginning of more— *how can a suicide—*
you won't allow yourself to even think flawed,
so crush the person you aspire to be. *trash compactor*
This is why you wear *end* *stop*
blankets when you're soaking *the end* *stop*
the sheets. Sweat makes you less
of a person. You're losing the weight. *not bad*
You're running out of places
to shove yourself, *and meds*
It already happened twice. *your end stopped*
So you'll file a schism and have
two places to keep your clay *schism*
because you have to find new *collisions*
and exciting ways
to hate yourself. You don't want to
be special but you have to,
because I'll end you if you're not special.
At least dress up *like a carpet,*
it's easier for people to know
you're here to be walked over.

II.

How can a suicide—it's madness.

Here's a tale of my fall, my fantasies:
where there was once darkness,
it is now deeper—
clinging skin to a rotting carcass.
This is my shadow.

Feel it.

Because I thought I would spawn

and desist in tangles
but I can count the many times
I've eaten dust, dirt, sand
on social islands only shouts
away and
my voice couldn't crack a fig.
I'd grant charisma to solitude
I've fallen up skyscrapers and into space,
I've drowned in pools of my own breath—
the years I've spent in a vacuum, a caricature
from mirrors of mirrors of mirrors.
I've traced the dotted line called horizon
and found mostly ice shelfs and extinction,
sheer cliffs I know I've thrown myself over
many times, hallowed times. The sound of my face is the sweetest
when smacked by a windshield.
Blindfolded, gun powder smells like cornbread
as if someone split the double barrel up my nose
instead of burying it in my mouth.
I've really only talked to people's feet and
I'm more balanced out of a tall, brown paper bag,
stalwart sleeping in a stairwell,
stuffing a cannon primed with my head.
I've crawled under trailer homes
because roaches are my favorite meal.

I've shouldered my way into burning buildings
knowing there was no one in there to save.
I'm a volunteer crash test dummy
and a stuntman vacationing in hell.
Take my blood, I'm honeymooning with malaria.
Rocks filled my pockets and walked me into the sea
Laying drunk on the streets of Baltimore.
My ear is in a time capsule
and I put my pillow in an oven.
I was to hold bait with my fingers as hooks.
It was a cactus, I held a cactus in my hand
and I squeezed it with my heart.

III.

How can a suicide be damned?
Though it's a dream gifted to you
to find new and exciting ways to hate
yourself, this was about more
than dying. This was about
finding ways to hold on. And everyone left.

And
it's my job to have faith in
my delusional apotheosis: that one
day, I'll be frisked, folded, spat
and reincarnated as
a god. How else can
I raise the dead, go back in time?
There's nothing left to shout.

I'll cram your smile in my wallet,
keep you in my backpack when

I road trip through the desert.
You're my favorite
bumper sticker and my warmest quilt.
I don't want to name you dear, it's
a candle scent already
taken. I'll be your bard instead.
I'll collect, I'll host, I remember
your dream to have a rare Martian cloud pass
through your entire body on
Olympus Mons. I'll give you
shit about that time you hit
my car with a golf cart or
your strange habit of standing
with your legs crossed. You sprinted
at the waves the first time you
saw the ocean surf, I was
running at your side. But I'll
never know why you bought those
coloring books and scribbled
out the images with a
sharpie or why you never
bothered to fight back, not once,
preferring to play the part
of the welcome mat. Even if
I can't convince you to stay
after I become a god
at least I'll have more places
to stow away what is left behind.

My Father Was a Carpenter

And I learned nothing of the sort
though I should have.
A sacrifice was made to live in the house instead of building it.
He said it was like bringing something back to life.
To walk through the carcass
season by season
reclaiming its flesh
from the black mold and shadows
and walking off the altar
back into the thicket.
Here, the ram comes in time at the binding—

****

Here, the coming of audio intrusions:
So with that—
with what I am
and the power it takes to silence
to shut my goddamn mouth
and the silence it takes to power
that, as I am
such with that
the arteries of archaic communiques
copper sinew and twisted
bob and weave through good bones
rip it out of the drywall
the dismantling
of what held together cul-de-sacs
we were crimped wire—
it follows
this silence
: and the quivering tremors left in the wake
: just breaths
on one end of a long-distance call, a call
meant to be— like bringing him back to life
and the way the dead of news is delivered:
dialing all the numbers at once
with a hammer—
thank God the power is out
and the night isn't helping either.

****

Smoke,
                    morphing black, unfolding itself skyward
a vehicle for heat.
And the noise   the possession we sacrifice
it hums orange
sirens, pleas, but mostly barking—   inconsiderate of funerals.
Perhaps the sidewalk chalk art sees
the left-behind mementos:
            chips in the wall from narrow corners and long couches,
            numerous carpet stains—indistinguishable now—but on shag.
            A portrait of Saturn unfolds itself down the canvas.
      The fire snatches every eye,   so
                  no one ever looks at the shadows
                              and what they've been doing
                                          for hours now.

****

Afterburn
smoke
from shadows
play   over the corners of the wall
giving the impression of mouth and speech.
But I know
it's rubble and what's left is
metal,   but almost
fake—   a gutter,
                metal screws
                              in place
and placate the deposits of squirrels
                              and conifers
                                          casting a downward glare
                                          from an upturned branch

in the family tree:
the genetics passed down from father to father to father
the longest cup,
floating
reservoir,
if not clean
dam
the squabble and drain it into the ground.
What does fighting over a will do to a house?
My mind is in the gutter
my knife has been the gutter
drenched in sacred red.
It's primitive,
the tool and the
sacrifices
upon the
altar
gutted.
The medication did not come in time.

PART II

PORTLAND

You may think it possible
to outrun this. All
you did
was move
the hamster wheel
to a prettier cage.

Door to Door

I don't get stressed from being busy. I get stressed by angry people, conflict, and when I am feeling trapped. I didn't know this yet. A few of my track teammates and I moved out to Portland after we graduated from college. Being unable to find a job trapped me in a financial struggle. I took anything I could get. I was an unarmed private security guard who biked my way around Portland at night to check on various properties. I was a sidewalk and public parks custodian. I was a commission-only door to door salesman of DirecTV in the age of streaming.

In order to motivate myself to make sales, since my income was dependent on it, I wouldn't allow myself to eat until I made a sale that day. If I didn't make any money from commission, I wasn't going to be buying much food anyway. But I used to eat unholy amounts of food. So this was rough.

Alongside the hunger, I began to feel like I was seeing people as dollar signs. I hated that. I hated that a person was reduced to ten minutes of calculated rhetoric for my own gain that possibly ended with me being able to eat. The calculation was no longer in the service for all good things for all good people. But even still, I forced myself to get very good at sales to stay afloat despite the cognitive dissonance. Afterall, I am a very good liar. However, soon my conscious would overtake my salesmanship. The stress of being unable to eat unless I pulled some Machiavellian stunts at the expense of others caused me to crack again. Of course, none of these jobs provided any kind of benefits or insurance, so medication or psych care was inaccessible.

The Bog

In a word, I am
Nihil
moves here.

I am the perfectly
wandering in by chance. They struggled
and

I gave them rest. I am the human floating, open eyes glinting in
sacrifices. I am the murderous dumping ground. I am the biome's

wronged. I am the don't bury
the depths. I am the lack of bird song: the putrid staleness solidified
in the air and the lifeless stare of the frog.
About me is

gnarling: the decay of life that preserves and
tints underground hale
the skin
of my mummified host and their dreams.

I am the time tear. Inside, madness is quiet, it does not disturb. It
is becoming of ripples, the last
bubble rising up
after a decade of *I am still*

here. I am the movement of time watched from
a church pew. I cover the regions of a heretic's prayer:

every termite-abused corpus. I am the lock and key on every

story you never wanted to hear. I am the willful stale.

I am a chorus of croaks, the snare   and drosera,
the landlocked doldrums, the melting clock, the symptoms' return.

Apoptosis

It's like something is eating
Our words
This is Portland
And I am a security guard pestering the homeless and addicted
I am becoming
Vaporous streams of carried tension
Lost in the smoke
Smoke substituting as people
People with recycled faces
Faces I ascribe names and meaning to
Meaning that unravels only to me:

Tyler only speaks when spoken to now
He's polite if he has to be
In my company
He used the smoke to label his bindings
Confinement to his tent under the overpass
Not lying, but a brokenness heavy enough to chain until
He cannot leave his tent, so I've taken it upon myself
To change his setting every day
For years, he hiked and photographed
I taped the photographs he kept to cement walls
Smoke drifted up from his mouth
Marking the places and times of memories
Until memories were not enough
Today, I have upgraded him to a circus tent
Red and white streamers line the overpass
Tyler has a picture of his father as a clown
He walked into furniture honking his horn
He lost his red nose in the pie Tyler threw when young
But it is time to drag him out of the tent
For a bar crawl and to be reminded of
The complexities of each patron

The workers comp case with Robert but
He's faking being injured, so he says to the bartender
Who politely nods and is unsure if he should laugh
But Robert isn't looking for it
He talks to fill the space of the dimly lit
The scuffed floors, dirty tables, seats with cushions
Who have been in a back-alley knife fight
The bartender checks to see if a glass is clean
Before filling it with liquid amber and sliding it down to Rachel
Whose obsession with hats
Has been the untimely death of various varmints
The furs of a skunk draped around the wide brim
We are in Portland indeed
This is pauper bliss
She licks her lips eyeing the glass
But we are lively still
Like we're bowling on the countertop
Like we dance on tables but also
Foaming at the mouth
Rabies, Rachel obviously
And the bartender can't stop the music
I grin and kick my feet up onto the table
Crickets aren't loud enough to be heard in this city
In addition to working security
I became a sidewalk custodian
And picked up numerous hypodermic needles,
Cigarette butts, and one time
I had to pick up human feces
Barehanded when my supervisor
Forgot to stock my station with gloves
Jim routinely sleeps in front of 6th Street church's entrance
When I'm wearing my security uniform
He knows I'll be by on my bike to wake him up at 3:00 a.m.
And ask him to unblock the access point
This is a ritual he doesn't mind

In fact, I think he looks forward to it
Once I wake him up, we talk
We talk about his daughter
Who he hasn't seen in years
But follows on Facebook using
His smart phone
For which he constantly has to find
Outlets in parking garages
So he can charge it and watch her succeed

The Custodian

Eyes   that could make a breeze softer
and crush cast-iron skillets, glancing back,
looking through the glass plane
                            upon a plane
they saw   a mortuary,
the unrecovered trapped at the dump,
splayed filth stings on the skin
and I'm sweating through meaning.
What fervor, what quilted landfill
does sight withhold
for those that want a peek
and why do my bones ring when they aren't soul?
Bearing the brew of the physical—it isn't gossamer, bring steadfastness
Compost my coda.   And the eyes!
Working hard and mushing your life into musings
that aren't your own, but you work
for it anyway   still   expecting results because
this   is the connotation of insanity
and I mop up the effort, spilt nectar on the floor, and don my gloves as
the janitor of the human race,
the devil that picks up after God.

Life Is Made Possible by the Lies We Tell Ourselves

Corkboard but more like brown napkins and paste
I try to harden it with memories. I tack pictures
Of friends and family, reminders urgent
For minding a reason for crawling day
By day out of the fiscal hole commission sink
Sinking morality and my spine is misaligned
Because I've been sleeping on the floor
Can't afford a bed but can afford prints
I wake from the shallow carpet
And stare at the ceiling to see the pictures I've hung too
I've learned from Tyler, I know
The potence of mnemonic aid
I see them smiling, I've made sure
To capture their best moments
An encouragement for me to live mine

I pretended myself a minimalist
To dodge questions about not having furniture
I convinced myself I'd eventually build my own

I posted motivational notes around the apartment

"I will fight even if I am beat
To live and die is not defeat"

I put sticky notes on my food to warn against eating
Not because of my roommates
But because I might steal my own food
It's stealing if I didn't earn it yet
To gain eating privileges
I had to knock on the doors
I had to sell the package

I had to reap the commission
It's the third day in a row without eating
I wake up to see pictures smiling down at me

"I will fight even if I am beat
To live and die is not defeat"

I am a hard worker
I am a hard worker
I will make it

It's not the slammed doors I need the pictures for
It's the people who let me in
The people who haven't had a human connection in months
Who tell me their stories while I look at my watch
I fell in a mud puddle
On the second loop around the neighborhood
It might evoke more pity
But all I think of is the microbes
I smashed in the fall

Today, I talked with a man who
Just learned
He was a father
Of a twenty-year-old son
He got a waitress pregnant on a cruise ship
And he never knew
I sold him DirecTV

Today, I prevented an elderly women
From running the lawn mower over her bushes
She might have had dementia
I definitely did
Not sell her DirecTV

Today, I was invited in to watch a documentary
The family thought it was important
That I knew the truth about vaccines
I sold them Cengage internet
When Netflix kept buffering

Today, I counseled a sixteen-year-old boy
Through his first break up
When he answered the door
But I made sure I talked to his mother
And sold her DirecTV

After three days of not eating
I sold so much I became
The second-highest ranked in sales
In the Pacific Northwest

"I am a hard worker
I am a hard worker
I will make it"

I am a liar
It's not the slammed doors I need the pictures for
It's the people I take advantage of
By pretending to be their friend

I brainwash myself to think
I am helping them by plating them a dish
I am not helping me
I am leaving these people
Better than how I found them

I am so distraught by the "that-a-boys" from the sales team
By the claps in the office

That I forgot
I earned
The right
To eat

Duane Street, Oregon City

I lived in what seemed like a haunted house. The warning signs were immediately obvious, almost comically glowing red flags. The house did not have a front yard. Instead of a front yard, the property was pressed against the side of Oregon City's Mountain View Cemetery. The oldest headstone is for an infant who died in 1847. It is a massive cemetery at one of the highest points in Oregon City, and as the name suggests, boasts a great view of Mount Hood when the area isn't buried under fog or low-hanging clouds. The sky seems very low when you're pressed up against it.

From the second-floor window of what would become the children's room, you can see a special part of the cemetery, dedicated in 2013, known as the Parents of Murdered Children (POMC) Memorial. The thought process for living here was that it meant the absurd West Coast property expenses might be marginally lessened. I was never making enough money. I never earned benefits that would provide the all-elusive, reasonably priced, buyer-no-beware healthcare.

The first day we moved into the house, the realtor was supposed to meet us there to give us the key. I will spend a lot of time looking at this door's keyhole. I saw someone looking out at me from the second-story window who I thought was the realtor already in the house waiting for me. He was an older, portly man with a pinstripe shirt and suspenders from what I could see from the window. We tried to open the door, but it was locked. So I knocked and I heard the man begin making his way downstairs to the front door. Then the realter pulled into the driveway behind us and the footsteps stopped. I was obviously confused about who was in the house but, go figure, nobody was. In horror movies, this is the point where the audience screams at the protagonists to not move into the house, but they do so anyway, common sense be damned. Our pit bull refused to go into the children's room for the longest time.

After I finished unpacking into the house, I realized I forgot my phone charger in my car. It was midnight and I just wanted to sleep after moving everything. But I knew my phone would be dead in the morning if

I didn't get it. I walked down the stairs and put my hand on the door. As I tried to turn my hand right, the handle refused and turned left. The house had decided it was keeping me inside. If I couldn't get out, I would peer through the keyhole and imagine every story I wanted to hear, building a whole imaginary world on the other side of that door.

Ghosts of Times

I keep thinking that the flowers
      the flowers
I write my dreams with
are going to die:

That   the stems laugh
the wither   black now running up my fingers   tangling
veins,   frayed   hairs   ignite, smelling
salts, wake
the caretaker.   He's gone.
Patches of foul
      smoke, sour
seismic tinnitus from the rupture—basalt flow.

The flowers
left in dreams are going to
      these hands
will glisten then   burn,
as the sweat
I once enjoyed would combust
on toil kerosene.   The ravage.
That woes would wrestle away wild
and tote fire kindles as currency.

And the fissures
In my skull   make it agony
      to think
since I've seldom needed to

choke
on my saliva   stifled through lahar
and cup it in the breadth of my hand,

there's life
in my spit and to even see it,
hear the millions calling
home.

Sleeping/Body Bag

I once witnessed a man screaming in the park.
He thought with wild eyes and projectile phlegm
that he was being consumed alive by an anaconda. But it was
black and faceless, with zipper teeth that were stitched together,
begging for a man to sleep inside its belly.

He yelled at me, pleaded with the snake to stop
but he kept pulling it up, his legs vanishing
into the maw. And when the snake had creeped
up to his chest, he breathed, "This is what God feels like,
isn't it?"

I heard this man a few days earlier, shambling
along with a rope of drool descending from his mouth
shouting, "I'll be free when you're all dead, better call
me while you can." You don't find this in movies.
You say, "This isn't a poem you're supposed to read on the bus."

I can't make up enough people, so in my cities
people recycle faces. That's when the shut eye
becomes the aggressor, when I divide myself
into pong thoughts of a backdrop and a billboard
for hours at a time.

Just listen here, when you and I pontificate on a bus about our
workday, we aren't finding ways to understand
each other's personal hell. And you switch topics because
this is uncomfortable, because I'm hinting at an illness
that I might say too much, but it's not like the news isn't either.
There's a man who throws dogs off a building for the fun of it.

No, no, no
don’t go to your phone for solace when someone could easily
talk about global warming and how none of our children
will know what a day without change feels like.
Our defiance is only a coping mechanism
and this is how you taste the mind without it.

Corneal Ulcers

It is here, leaning against a tree at the park
as the car drives away,
and I, holding their empty suitcases,
have come to know an adopted
vision
of apocalypse
grafted by social services
    sticking   branches
into my corneas.
The red veins slipped off my eyes and wound themselves up the crisp—
functional visibility—
soon flower petals blossom as auditory intrusions,
as scenic interruptions.
I know their scent, possibly   roses and
grasping to touch, understanding, until certain
the thorns sprouted down the branch and out of my eyes:
the possibility
of hanging—no, I mean having
the children taken away
because I am getting more
sick.

And what power against the grain—
but before my foot   roots
I walk into walls between park and road,
jam wood in—

                                                            to further

sit in this present darkness, somewhere
and smooth the velvety petals, which my fingers,
finest grain sandpaper.   And roots—
Eventually,
the retinal branches

will grow
the bleeding roses
beyond my reach,
to which my fingers,
Left strafing in the crisp—

Actually
these aren't
roses
they're spiders.

Mt. St. Helens

On a trip up Mt. St. Helens on the day after New Year's, I saw something incredibly unnerving. The drive to Mt. St. Helens is long and winding, through sparsely populated Pacific Northwest towering forests and around some alpine lakes. From Portland or Vancouver, it takes around an hour of prolonged road sickness from the dips and winds. But that view is something.

The road mostly travels up the south side of the volcano, the side still intact after the eruption. The north side is less traversable thanks to the massive crater created when the mountain blew its lid. Pre-1980, the mountain was nearly 10,000 ft. tall. Its current elevation is 8,300. It quite literally blew its lid. The force of the explosion shattered these massive trees, fragments still visible.

Due to snowfall earlier that week, I was not able to fully make it to the top of the mountain, but on the way up, I arrived at a tree graveyard. Either from the force of the explosion, fire prevention, or the logging industry, almost all of the trees on this jutting patch of mountain had been removed. What was left in having no home: thousands of stumps, headstones that told the birth and death dates with tree rings rather than with math. I stayed here for a while as a cloud silently collided and ran through me and up the mountain side. It's not Olympus Mons, but it was something. The ground was black where there wasn't snow. It looked like a fungus, like black mold.

I sat on a headstone breathing in clouds and imagined all of the life that these trees once hosted. Soon, the cloud passed and the sun reemerged, warmth flowing over the area. My clothes began to get inexplicably wet. I stood up and realized the stump I was sitting on was emitting vapor. I looked around me and all of the stumps began to steam. Wisps of mist like ballerina arms rose, coiled, uncoiled, and fell before rising again, like the souls of the trees were dancing. They weren't fighting their death; they were dancing with it. Hundreds of wooden graves opened, and the spirits of the trees made the air vibrate and shimmer. The ground became less hard and more damp as my trail shoes softly sank with each step. Though there was no sound, my brain gladly provided the absent stimulus. It is likely that you, like me, can imagine the sound of vapor, or the sound of cloud collision, or the sound of damp; however, these things don't emit any sounds themselves. I heard hissing and whispering though there was barely any wind—the playfulness of the long dead ready to wake up and stretch.

Everything is Fine

Rhythms and fruit and shimmer I am certain of foster the space for forgiveness needed to scratch music back on the board, one heavy nail screech at a time, one or two blistering ear drums for every note remade, redeemed, and yet there is no forgiveness without acknowledgment, only adherence to the preestablished plastic fruit artists use to paint so they can take as long as they like because plastic has no time limit, fraudulence no abiding code, plastic apples might as well be eternally recurring garbage; but the real apples I hold in my outstretched hand—that I plated for you, that I cut for you, that I smothered in caramel for you—oxidize before my eyes while your teeth dig into the waxy absurdity of "I'm fine," the perception that everything difficult is practice done once and hung up in a museum, still fine and unchanged when it's clear that paintings are meant to have layers, meant to be coated again and again, strokes this way and that, with new colors and striking revisions.

I paint images of rotting fruit using the guts and mold they leave behind.

Saturn Devouring His Son

An indiscriminate hunger eats
whatever it can snatch—marvel
at the kind of guts it takes
to bury children
in his throat. His outsides
are in. A gullet
capable of cramming
the human arm into
moist darkness
as the esophagus massages
the chewed arm on its way down
into the bile and acid
Goya splashes on the plaster wall—alone
in a house for years
greeted by Kronos
every time he walks down the first-floor hallway.
It's just his insides
but out. How long
would he stare
into the bulging eyes of the titan
to paint it like his child on the wall.
It's just a god but inside out.

Bullous Myringitis

With the children
gone, winter
was all it took
to imagine
a sound
I've never heard :

What unbeknownst
prophet would imbed
by accident
into the making
of clay pots—

: a sound, an auditory intrusion
and all the life grafted to the harmony
of bark clipped, sap dripped, leaves adrift :

—left and gone,
by millennia, a prophet holding his ear to heaven
clutches it in pain.
The potter turned prophet records it all
in the grooves of the clay
a stylus can find the cries—

: now dissonant
to the violence of collapse,
strain, weight, and crack
amplified by every tincture of ice and what weight before the thaw :

—of blister welts
and open sores drying on the nearby drum—

: and anticipating the sound

of a tree in Portland
coming through my roof
a branch of sequoia
impaling me as I sleep
and termites and spiders
hopping off the limb,
legs like conifer needles falling in the bed,
to greet the red warmth I call ruin :

—sheets stretched taut so every pus sack
can be heard exploding, leaking, and the membrane
lilting back down, overextended, useless—

: sound, all of it,
put simply,
a splinter of life falling from the sky.
Every sound, a shatter of glass holding in what makes a home.
And every sound is what transforms the deaf night into powerlessness and
:

—outage, the prophet's ear, failed.
What apocalypse can God whisper to the human ear?
Can a prophet look upon the face of God
and not be blinded by—

: the light that was shown for me, now routed.
Roads that were open to me, now blocked.
And the intense quiet before another
explosion of wood de-shingling
the roof of :

—the heavenly and all of its workings
like vibrations in the cochlea.
Pulses of air
known to the touch, understanding, until certain—

: a car was stabbed by the makings
of an elegant cane hidden in apocalypse
bearing the tangle of the rest of the tree. :

—of life
given to clay
and to hear clay speak
of what it gained and what is—

: Gone
with the children,
winter, all it took was :
—a fresh sound—

Getting Out of the House

I sometimes had delusions that I could see the future. When I was having manic episodes, I would go to the grocery store and stand inside for hours. I would pretend that I was shopping, but I was just pushing my cart from aisle to aisle aimlessly. If I concentrated hard enough while wandering, I could leave my body and look down, as if I had become the ceiling fluoresce high above. From the top down, I would try to predict the paths of every person in Fred Meyer. And each person would get their own prediction chart on which items they were shopping for. I guessed based on their clothing and my fabricated memories. I convinced myself I could read them, what they were going to buy, when they would be back. I convinced myself I could influence them through being conscious of their movements and the mathematics of calculated moment.

By this point, the delusions and hallucinations made it hard to sell things door to door. I quit the security job, the cleaning job, and the sales job. I worked for Two Men and a Truck and then a solar company and quit that too once I got accepted into an MFA program. I hated quitting and believed I needed to be punished for doing it so frequently.

Eventually, I started working in a care facility for those with Alzheimer's and dementia while in the MFA program. There is irony here. This way, I didn't always seem like the most distraught person in the room.

Drip

There were two men. Scenic interruptions.
No, three
Holding
Me down
Striking
Matches
Wearing night glasses and displaying their master plan
On an Etch A Sketch
Conversations gurgled salt water through grinding teeth telling me to—
They tied me to a
German Shepherd
Who was tied to a tree
They seemed to trust him more than—
And the ceiling was lightning stars and the grass—
The beefy blond one slapped me
Said I shouldn't look too closely at my—
The grass   What was going on with—
My hands folded then
My wrists and my elbows and my shoulders and my—
The German Shepherd licked my face
Said it was my last warning
The grass had grass growing along its ridges in fluorescent green fractals
I have never felt
Out of control
I ate the Twizzlers
Tethering me to the German Shepherd
The five men pounced on me and held me down waving the matches
They held them to their faces and their faces
Dripped into mine

Everything Is Fine II

Why do I feel nothing? Why are the walls talking to me? Why are spiders crawling out of people's eyes? Why are the ghosts of murdered children wandering around my house?

The doc, chewing gum, eyebrows askew, forehead slightly creased, hummed passively at my confession. "Have you been getting enough sleep?"

Let me ask you this, doc. When you and the boys stay up a little late throwing back cold ones while watching the Seahawks get their asses handed to them, and you stoically shed a single tear muttering, *"Maybe next year."* And, as a result, you maybe get four—no, three—hours of drunken sleep before shambling into this office. When you are sleep deprived like that, do you hallucinate? Do you identify with my inability to feel because your football team lost a game?

"Well, have you been drinking enough water?"

Why is there a goddamn gatekeeper barring me from proper care? Aren't you people supposed to be afraid of me without my meds? Why did this visit cost me triple digits? I can't afford insurance!

I get Occam's razor, I truly do, but maybe we can skip some standard procedure and go right to the part where you get me into seeing a psychiatrist.

Because I am seeing people's faces drip into mine.

When I couldn't get on the schedule for proper psych care, I went to inpatient for hallucinating and some scary compulsive thoughts that I will take with me to the grave. But this is Portland, and I don't look like your average crazy person. The team questioned me; I told them what was going on.

"Well, have you been experimenting with any harmful substances?"

No, I have not been taking any goddamn drugs.

"You seem a little stressed, but you should be fine in a couple of days."

And they sent me on my way.

Everything is not fine.

Like Needles

I spent time as a watchdog
But without teeth
Bicycle around Portland
In uniform but unarmed
And tell the homeless they couldn't
Sleep underneath the awning
They were blocking the entrance
With their exhausted bodies
Watching them is like
Intravenous injections by proxy
Sometimes empathy is dangerous
Falling from the sky
Sky like proxy
And the authority to govern what we know as blue
Like stained glass
Like crystal meth
There are mice shitting in my garage
Eating my old files
Like a lunchbox, they carry the bits with them
Like the plague and how that saying goes
Like my friend Tyler who dropped dead last week
He couldn't handle it
And the toxicity that turns blood to sludge
Like needles
I want to structure parables
Like there is an architecture, an ocean wave
Of truth, musings made to sound
Gavel, govern a sky uprooted to tumble and waterfall
The anecdotes of   The vignettes of   The rhymes
The tall tales
And swan songs
Echo to fade, tumble to waterfall
Needles sow the type

Script the fate of those that use them
I poke holes in the amendments
Inverse braille—blind for between the lines
In all the wrong places, the court sees
How the law is to be upheld, how parables
Of ox gorings are meant to prevent
Future ox gorings, but an ox doesn't know the law
But the deaths stay the same, felt, down
Soft as edged glass, stained
Like crystal meth
Outstretched arms in firmament armistice
The right to bear arms
Purple with veined scars
Syringe deposits on the curb, bone piles in a bear cave
My eyes are on it again, again
Water, water, water, water
Where is it
Sometimes I can see the surface and maybe there's a "one last time"
They say softly as I urge them to move their makeshift shelter
One last time
To shoot up with water instead and flow the stand of time
Still the banks of river
God in the chemistry, chemistry is a law
Cardboard blankets enough to drudge winter's end
Sweet agony of withdrawal with glimmering eyes hope
In the hypodermic
Move past again and again and again and again
Constantly dying
But there's life in that
Keep living, living, lvng, lvn
Again * again again gather
Again again * again all *
Again * again again * great *
Age * gain * addled * adage * again

** * * *** * * * ** ** *

This is winter
On a bad itinerary
I am not taking any goddamn drugs
But these people
Being deposited here
At the inpatient facility
Definitely are
Coming down
And as I watch them shoot up
I make a joke:
I * don’t * need * drugs * to * hallucinate

As witches gather in the red ink
Loose their veins from their forearms and
Bind me to a pulpit of searing horn
Make me watch them sharpen an axe
The floor is thrashed meat
The red ink boils on the ceiling
Bubbles into the eyes that drop to the ground
Cathedral of broken glass, scraped bone archway
Buttress point to the ground
Holes boil in the thick hair called walls—inverse braille
Chandeliers of amalgam flesh sprout from the floor
And measured line of horizon topples
Gravity like waterfall and I’m upside down again
Witches walking on the ceiling fill the hanging pews
Saturn shambled into the cathedral with a foaming mouth
When Berlioz first started playing this piece in concert hall
It is said some people would flee into the streets
During the “Dies Irae” portion.
It’s plausible enough for me.
Somehow he captured what dread sounded like
And Goya painted it on his walls

Atmospheric Entry

Though I am told to leave the facility, I'm still losing my mind, and I saw a shooting star for the first time in my life, watched as it made love to our atmosphere with enough rug burn that it superheated and splintered, fragments branching off into their own arcs and stories and destinations that they will never be able to communicate with the whole after their blaze finally fizzles out—light up the night sky for a moment and hope someone witnesses you on the way down:

PART III

THE TRUTH WAS MEANT TO SET YOU FREE

Sometimes, when I speak,
I see language breaking
but you can still see
the meaning in it,
right?

And if That Is What Breaks You

Buyer beware of the pumpkins jostling about and ripple-edged butting the junk scattered around my trunk.

Buyer beware of the midnight ecstasy, the high fluoride toothpaste, bristles that draw the slightest drip-drip from my receding gums.

Buyer beware of the mistletoe dangling from a low-hanging branch above gravestone so lost in names that lichen has filled in the creased stone where meaning of chisel once hammered away.

Buyer beware of the grief and Splenda dustings clinging to the edges of a shit mug holding shit coffee. It's okay, we reasoned. The coffee is for people who the world has forgotten.

Buyer beware of the squeaky wheels carrying the ancient geriatric sarcophagi din, hollowed eyes, loose nightgowns, and tight spittle crusted to places drool should never reach.

Buyer beware of the lifetime you shred and how that prized squelping corrugation in your skull will maggotize into highways of crisscrossing larvae.

Your reality is not as real as always, concrete minus the rebar, holding but solidly less unshakable, the blow of a pick and the crumbling scree overturns all notions of stability.

I hear the thuds of pumpkins rolling around as I drive to work at the memory care facility after leaving my psychiatrist's office.

My teeth are the first signs that the body is not abstract, only obtuse, and only borrowed, half-lives narrate the eaves and creeping, so much so that I now measure minutes with the count of every chomp and grind of the slow chewing dead-eyed Gerald masticating on the cud of time.

I walk about in the clothing of ghosts, discarded garments on the racks of Goodwill, good for me, wallet is light and the clothes are worn, now and forever.

I recognize some of the clothes from the patients I care for and the time they bide, their families pining ,watching while the erosion of dementia settles in the room like magma, the cold laminate tiles are no match for the colon bags and the reverse afterbirth of lingering chemo administrations. I just hope they don't recognize who I'm wearing.

I wash dishes.

I wash dishes and sometimes I get so lost in Simple Green and suds and nibbled bits, slop, and the amalgam of rejected steamed vegetables that I don't think about Gerald chewing.

I look up from the dishes to see the wheelchair-bound Gerald, his mouth hanging open and jaw slightly unhinged, wearing a floral bib spattered with an orange puree, the sidelined mush that we once called sweet potatoes.

And in Gerald's mind, and mind only, as he can no longer talk, sweet potatoes were once served alongside the corn he harvested that day, dinner plates full from the sweat of the brow, the earth sacrificing a bit of it for a bit of him, he sacrificing a bit of his back's lifespan for the sustainment of his family, so that his giddy children could grow into stern adults and place him in a memory care facility.

That too is a sacrifice—buyer beware, it somehow costs $5,250 a month to keep dear, old Gerald out of a cemetery, but just barely, no matter how nice the facility, he's taking walks around the perimeter of a graveyard, sneaking a peek with the utmost yearning when his roommate hops the fence. This experience costs nearly a mile in dollars per month.

My grandpa on my dad's side lived out most of his end days in a facility just like this. Except Grandpa Jones had schizophrenia. But he liked to walk, and the facility restricted his walking. In protest, he broke out of the facility by yoinking someone's coat off a hanger, flipping up the collar, and somehow walking unnoticed out the front door. My aunt told me that he walked twenty miles from Chicago back to his wife and children in a snowstorm. He didn't have shoes on. And when he made it home, he was sent right back.

I don't know why people who are breaking or already broken walk without shoes on.

My grandpa on my mom's side suffered from similar deterioration in the last years of his life caused by Lewy Body Dementia. It might have been a mercy that Papa didn't have it long enough to end up in a place like this. He died in hospice.

I don't bother to put on deodorant. Alzheimer's takes your sense of smell first.

I handle a population that can go at any minute in a time where a new disease like COVID is a letter that was lost in the mail finally being answered.

When I'm home, there are flashes of half-covered teeth in a terrified grin as I swing the children around the room in their costumes. Pumpkins on the table ready to visit the mortician, where we will cut them open, the pumpkins, take out their guts, and give them a pretty face for the funeral attendees to remember them by. A face glowing with light for an hour while everyone silently prays the face doesn't cave in on itself when it's their turn to approach the coffin for candy.

It doesn't pay to use metaphors that way.
Sometimes.
I dream of plastic bag mausoleums
And the strangle hold
the resistance to break down and decay,

that something that kills even the oldest turtle in the ocean will retain its form for perhaps another thousand years as it floats around in the current—

—

—I can hear the ghosts of murdered children complaining
how dirty
the house
they haunt—

There are questions I don't bother asking such as whether or not the people I care for are aware of where they are and what is happening to their brains.

There are truths I don't bother telling them, like how the sweet potato farmer's wife has been dead for six years now. That's actually a lie. He has been told, but he has forgotten.

It is said that since they cannot remember processing traumatic news such as the death of a spouse, that each repeated telling of the news is like hearing it for the first time, and then they have to process it, grieve it, and learn to exist again as a broken person before forgetting their loss and continuing life, still broken but unsure why.

It is said that the reality of inevitable death is not something one ever fully grasps, and since the beginning of recorded history, humans have been obsessed with finding a way to escape aging. From the *Epic of Gilgamesh* to Daoist practitioners confident that mercury was an elixir of everlasting life, and that drinking it would not only indefinitely prolong their lifespan but would also offer them communion with the celestial beings.

I cannot speak as to whether or not they talked with gods, but I can confirm that they are very, very dead.

It doesn't pay, buyer beware,
to tell the truth,
as in, I will be
terminated for not giving them

lies and affirmation
that reality as they know it
still exists,
that loved ones long dead
still live
that this facility is not a cold, dead place
that logic, reason, spirituality,
can nullify pain or at least
offer a means to understand
that I am constantly dying,
that balding, sore backs, increasingly frequent
doctor-, psychologist-, psychiatrist-demanded
checkups are absolutely necessary,
that I might already be in a care facility
reliving my life again and again in an eternal recurrence
drifting from one reality to the next.

—I do not have
        the motivation
        to pick up all of this
        garbage—

I compulsively sniff things I know smell bad to make sure I haven't lost my sense of smell. Lucky me, my armpits are quite ripe from stress sweat.

I am aware that there is a point of acceptance that most terminally ill patients stumble upon while their family still rages against the world, spinning over a thousand miles per hour.

Gerald will try to choke himself with solid food. On purpose. It's the reason his sweet potatoes must be liquified.

I chew with my mouth closed, not because I am polite or considerate. Because I am not. I chew with my mouth closed so no one can see that I am eating solid sweet potatoes.

I am oh so aware that the symptoms for those on the schizophrenic spectrum are a stone's throw away from presenting as dementia or Alzheimer's. On a practical level, I work here because I need the simple green. Subconsciously, this is a preparation ritual: a parent biting his tongue before his son goes in for circumcision.

I can't talk for hours after wiping Gerald. He turned his bewildered head around and made eye contact with me while I checked the toilet paper's contents for blood. I saw my face reflected in his eyes and he saw his face in mine. Both expressions are unspeakable. I will be him and he was me. We will wait for the day when this becomes
unspoken,
mechanical,
impersonal.

It has to, or it will—

There's a certain kind of multi-leveled irony of a middle-aged caretaker with a tambourine cheerfully coercing the lyrics of John Denver's "Take Me Home, Country Roads" out of those who are now forced to live in a memory care facility. I believe she thinks this is an attempt to liven their spirits. She should have picked a different song.

I watch because I have to.

And what of it
the chipped paint—a portcullis to every anxiety
housed in the walls?

And I have wondered if there are
perhaps people, things
which can shift
shift, falter, stumble
into another reality
and come out on the other side unscathed, a dream barely remembered:

—plastic cups
        and the oblong, multi-colored pharmaceutical gifts they contain,
        untouched by erosion, unlike me—

And the wake-up shatter shock,
there are cursed
                        feet in these hallways.
They are the feet that wander
and a medical plan that prevents restriction
since my grandpas, both of them, were literally prescribed to wander.
I'm guessing that making the facility into a circle was a practical choice.
My grandpas scarcely had a scenic interruption when they were permitted to walk.

These cursed feet that now visit me
on a long, barefoot walk down the genetic line
with a mixture of pity and shame.
It is now called the Jones Pace,
restless walking until you get yelled at
for wearing down the carpet with your stupid, dirty bare feet.
Why do we dislike shoes so much?

—what is your woe? Great Pacific Garbage Patch.
        I have to capitalize it
        like the garbage
        is a deity since it will most certainly outlive the worship of numerous gods.
        How do you come back—

It is always a guessing game
if they can bear to see a pillar of strength
reduced to a weakened state
and the bets are on who will turn away first
which family members will stop visiting.
Wishing they should have been home yesterday, yesterday.

—it's the texture of gizzard
    this baggage soup, alphabet salad
    waywardness in a Campbell's can—

It's cursed feet
that administer
every
   little
     blessing:
           the tidings of churning pharma.
The tight hold and around we go,
up, down, back around,
"That doesn't work."
"Nope, not that."
"Here, try this."
Medication like pumpkin seeds
    with a raw spittoon welcoming
my mouth is
     leaking suds. Simple Green can't make everything green.

This visitor wants to know what the drug is called
but naming drugs is like throwing a dart at a board of letters
and there's no way to remember what you were last prescribed
or what comes next.

—it's like a foghorn in the doldrums
 And the sky matches the horizon matches the ground. An endless sea of
 garbage and plastic apples. Plastic is older there, older than the trees—

Sometimes I think correct punctuation is a vain attempt to hold back entropy. If I am honest, my thoughts are not punctuated. The authentic me is uncontained and scrambled. That's the problem. Punctuation is a scabbed wound that I keep picking at.

After being undiagnosed for years, I finally received one before I came into

work: schizoaffective disorder with obsessive/compulsive tendencies. Knowing the name didn't help. Instead of just incremental periods of madness, instead of demonic possessions, instead of a haunted house, it is just that my brain will be wrong for, more or less, always. Knowing the name of an illness isn't a cure. I had to feign happiness to my psychiatrist who gave the diagnosis like we solved a cold case. They're still dead bodies; it doesn't matter if the children's killer has been apprehended. If I am to believe my family history, a diagnosis like this is a very long death sentence at best. If I am to believe the news, I will lose myself and turn to violence. They're still bodies, it doesn't matter if the children's killer has a sensationalized diagnosis. As I wash dishes in the kitchen, all I can hear are the Denver lyrics transforming to match my telos.
Take me home,
country roads.
There's no place
where I belong.

—and if that is what breaks you—

*

Despite the fantasies * *

* * I have never *

* * attempted * *

* * suicide * * *

* * ** but this * *

* * * * * * * **

** * * * * ** * * ** * ** * ** *

this is unmaking

distinction
is not

a character trait
it is
a sin to blame God—
the lies
we tell ourselves
—for life to go on
for there to be an exit sign
reserved for those that work here
awaiting
quiet
sense-making lives
built like bricks in a wall
and walled us in
we chip away
paint from the inside
so we can put our mouths to the portcullis
and scream

—at this moment, at least I can be thankful
that I can still smell the garbage—

what studies may come
and answer
everything we would like to know
about the schizophrenic spectrum
have I become
the lock and key
on all the stories
you never wanted to hear
I am told I cannot talk
about this diagnosis
I am told people will
not understand
I am told I will be
shunned

but I don't understand either
and I need to talk to
someone
please
tell me what is real—

Do you take your pharmaceutical Eucharist with apple sauce?
Or can you bear it dry?

—before I become this

Unravel

Hello, I've dug a quarry in your mind
I've broken you down
and we need to excavate
we need to make an effort
to punctuate now
it's trauma and spite and lingering will
that commands me
run, Forrest, run
it's a foghorn blasting contagion of the poisoned—
it's
it's a terrible and dreadful thing to become
that of future pauper bliss and a listless un-redemption
unmaking of hope
and a comfort knowing you'll never be better
not enough to Adam
not the naming privileges
name this becoming
by summarizing a life into one word
No
you pauper
punctuate No
this is how language breaks
there is someone unborn and he needs a name
No
Atlas
No
I picture him
fully grown
knowing the meaning of that name.
No
and all of the people he'll let down
No
punctuate

I am trying!
—he's no longer splashing sky on the canvas
out of room, thankfully the walls are white.
Atlas—something is already
;mid-gone,
something is already

:_________________________
____
____

That is something!
A parting of somethings
like several endings in—falls short

every nomination falls short
every sublimation.
A subway crashes at 11:56 a.m. into
cigarette smoke that is something!
Bent neck and the compressed
cartilage.
As if,
I,
as I am,
hopped off the subway at just the right moment
I will
arrive to greet the person who stole my car.
I decided I would name my son Atlas
in a future
that I didn't—
wish to happen
so I could wrap the idea in tinfoil and light it on fire
and hope the fire doesn't spread—
swirling mists, visible thanks to the stark green—
this is a graveyard tree

piercing a cloud in the spring:
the sky is so low without him.
As if I as I am, keep the not-real things as scaffolding
and my eyes will fight to be
that way—what I do
in the swirling mists.
I know
what I do
with kindling
it can't be fooled
something!
ultra sound
there's the feet
there's the hand
that is
This is a future I rejected:
I came to the car thieves to find
the kind of nature needed for apathy.
I can't seem to twist empathy fatigue into nature.
But we can't think like nature
it has no need of us.
I assume human emotions of a branch
of an Atlas
even the wall and weight
somehow the bricks have wrinkled—
even our dandruff
will hit the ground
with the smack of a skyscraper
becoming a missing person report.
It's on the same desk as the stolen car report.
I named my becoming Cain and I walk the earth
and the earth
is not forgiving
of those who walk. Or those who walk away.
Chill and rain linger even
in the skin cells
I've left behind
and my hair mirrors my actions
flailing, fall-out, and one day reflective

of the overcast sky.   I chew gum to keep
my mouth shut. Don't get me wrong,
I am not ungrateful for winter
—it keeps my hands in my pockets
and off my phone.   That is something!
My number has changed and I
don't feel
the need to let anyone know, though
I am becoming   : ungrateful
: the Scripture
I will ignore and
activate; my actions repeat
and are
repeated with cyclic testament as I
am someone who would sacrifice after
being sacrificed.
Yokes, whips, and the beast of burden
I am becoming
hauls tenfold my weight up the
steep   concealing my house. It's prophets,
as I climb,
all of them
shouting
the father is dead, the worms are left.
I was told the worms have grown wings and now
challenge the birds, but our wings will never
have feathers.
We'll always look more like bats.
And consequences. And
I am becoming contrapasso
when weight
is detached from
mass
and I am
disassociated

from me.
I am the
enemy I grew up
despising:
A statistic.
It's clear as sky the tidal mist and mists
and fallen
night
in midday
and yes, the moon's shadow is heavy when with your own darkness
you are the smite with your own darkness
and the smitten with your own
darkness
when it used to be your light.
Because I changed. I became change
when I promised
I never would
to scores of people in a rotting hometown
in an Atlas
lost in the trunk
with its own darkness
and the car was stolen!
These people in my Atlas who seemingly moments ago
showed kindness in unparalleled yet
insignificant ways.
Dusted my back— It's these moments— Why can't I think of more—
tucked my shirt tag in— kindness I didn't— am I ungrateful—
called me out of the blue— that brings me to tears— that is something!
None of them
asked for permission asked for
I'm papier-mâché
but I'm confused if the hollow inside is not entropy
it's still dark and
even entropy
has a use unlike

the outdated plastic grocery bags I am becoming
and one of their two fates:
landfill
or tumbleweed.
They glide by my fathering gait
and what's left that will always be
left: the scar tissue
planetwide
and the muck and flotsam populating
the collective human soul. The Garbage Patch. The soul who knows
what it means to succumb under
the smile
through beatings, the pulled teeth
out of that smile the lashings the wedges between
my fi n g e rs
cut with tin snips
the wedges between
my fa t h e rs
the genetic will
and so I am vanished and eat the vanished as
I am becoming
rock-bottom feeder
what I eat is what I find left:
I eat
the rocks and I am
becoming them, the rocks, :shells of a carcass [ ]
But limestone,
not sturdy,
just looks the part.
I find ice cream on the sidewalk
and you know what
I eat it
off the well-trodden filth
yet it still tasted like ice cream
with a hint

                    of roadkill.
My bloodshot eyes bleed to judge
                         ice cream the color of roadkill.
          I have a frenzied fantasy of becoming a
     roadkill
     squirrel under someone’s tire, a buck in the crosshairs
the fathers who pull the trigger   the fatherless finding unmaking corpses
          blood fever never broke plight
of the insentient
victims trapped between a colossal march and
                         the especially deep
          furrows away the malignant stains
twisted branches,
          more tracks
                    no tracks anymore.
Bloody roadsides, smeared corpses
for accidents. Or was it
             was it? Because I thought you wanted that suicide fantasy.
Drag back the kill
          by the antlers
     for fun
blood is that all things are permissible
but not all things are
                “beneficial.”
This dream sings to me
                              that is something!
Bloodshed
          is the chew, spit, and smoke
gnashing of crops and threshing teeth
                            ravaged,
bled,
     grown,
          cultivated,
                bled again and bled their kin—
so I can live this blood I am becoming:

hail
        when I once fell
                        like snow.
My anger gets the best of me   the best of me
I beat
                        my chest and throw my
            |
            |
fist through a chiasmus just to show
            |
            |
                                that I
                                can still fight
something
            if I can't fight myself that I am becoming.
Remember the horror
            of what we create.
I am become death, destroyer of somethings.
And the role of the father. But I am not
the flash
        I am
the cancer
            I am the cancer
                                I am the cancer
              I am the fall-out
            I am the slow
            genetic
            death sentence
            my son potentially has.
        I whittle away
their lives from the inside
                                because I am lonely and need more
papier-mâché.
        And I am becoming rock bottom
where I piss in the shower because the toilets

are broken and I'm on pilgrimage
                                        from my own house.
I cackle
                when I'm mad, throw myself
        up the stairs,
I pass the door in the children's room
                and get a whiff and I know
        there's shit and sometimes life
is such that I   just shut the door.
And I am becoming this cold, the
        sideways rain
and the branch snaps and the roof
collapse and the chimney
                    is still there, so of course
                                                    it's wrinkled brick
        and that's coming down too
lying broken in the yard
                                        on my dead grass
and on aftermath and subterfuge shouted
down from the stratosphere by a winter microburst.
My illness has been condemning
                    the sun   for a decade. I took a role not knowing
I could
                        rend happiness from lives.
I am becoming a role model for a
role I feel
            the imposter. Impersonator.
I mime
            childrearing
   through a stern look
or a thumbs up.   At best
                    I read

like a newspaper, at worst a C
R
On-word
S
ChiasmuS
S
Way-word
O
R
D.
If I am doing anything right
sarcasm
is fluent by second grade

:______________________________
____
____

if I am doing anything
write
the subway ride must come to an end.
Drop my unmade unbecoming slop
leftover pig trough slime
splattered
on the door
seeping into the keyhole
this keyhole
millions of years
in the making. The edge
of rock grounded to stars.
Can I
unlock this?
Can I talk about all the stories
I've need to hear,
I've needed to tell?

But there's been a boot on my throat for so long.
These waves ripple their
conjunction
of tectonic battering rams.
This ragged continent at large can't
yet
swim to this stone stoop,
this archway,
this portal
to a future rocked away
by a keyhole held by my youngest daughter's ghost,
cradle—it always smelled
like raspberries,
jelly phlegm dangling from her tiny chin; dotted,
but sometimes
splashed on her bib.
I can't
bring her
to the beach yet,
it's too hard
to push a stroller on the sand.
Trouble is, it's not when the backdrop summits topple
and we fall~
~
~
~
~out of our high chairs
and need nine stitches, it's when everything is poised
swimmingly and I am still hollowed out
boulder hallowed,
the Pacific salt polishes me
smoother, like it always has before:
in that million-year past, I knuckle-drag
a grove
with atmosphere-smushed trees—there's a crest

for anhedonia. When it's not a tide and
the wet brine and stick
simply rolls. And the sky is so low without them.
My daughter
is millions of years in the making
and soon I can bring her before
bring her
when she can toddle
and tumble with the sand to
cushion the fall. I'm glazed for stone legs,
limbs I can't find:
no one
runs from this,
you get a perch.
I can't be there now to stop
her from wandering
into the undertow.
I'll hope
from a trench in my heart
and she'll float on with the breeze
gliding onward
where she can
forget voiceless
summers where suffering
starts to feel good,
where my solstice
sprints
like mad into the past, replaced by howls
and lengthened time spent gazing at
the falling stars through fogged breath. Why would I,
why would I
want to become this becoming? I once thought
the darkness only comes when you search
for a light and find
unbecoming.

That we spend so much
of our lives asleep
because being awake
is too taxing.
Our ears have heard so much that
it all stops
having meaning and the drums
that beat our senses into submission—
and look,
audio crumbles altogether.

I am tall, but that means my time here
will be shorter, since I have more
of me that can go wrong.
But something tells me, I am becoming: short
and should try to live
: taller.

Dog-ear that place
I've read, that moment
I suspended entropy
and I could swear
I knew what the end
of attrition tasted like.
A family, standing there, I'm hoping
saying nothing was enough
to unmelt the clock, to hold it smiling,
marbleize a breath in time.
It just made my hands sweatier.
The chapter is becoming but,
not yet,
as if, I as I am
still left
a pen in the crease
one day again to scribble in the margins
when it's the day and we together
of highest noon sprint into tall grass

and nothing basking in the shimmer
has a shadow of Lahaina noon.
A contrapasso is having time
and waiting instead
knowing the ghost of my oldest daughter
has a strange world of grey lines

:______________________
____
____

staring her down
and in a moment she may be broken
and everyone shrugs their shoulders saying
What? You didn't see this coming?
No!
I don't want to. Please stay
five so I can pick you up and make you walk
on the ceiling. The ceiling is so low without them.
You pauper!
No, a liar.
I am becoming
father and I've known them all.
I am
the curse the ghosts of my sons will say
for giving them an irrational fear
of leftovers.
Or clogged toilets.
I am
the warmth they'll remember
when they see a pile of blankets
left over
expecting me
to rise out of it shouting,
I am the blob!

And tackling them
into a pillow fort.
Remember curiosity experienced, tinkering with wonders
unclasping, unlocking
destroying, remaking
watching a world becoming
entangled with life.
Remember that sweetness, a cure, for your son's temper
is to ask him for help
or tell him you're hurt
and watch how quickly he
forgets himself.

And my unborn
I will become something
for you too.
I want to promise you will
never see what I came from
only what I begot.
And it won't be Atlas.
And I'll hang
this becoming on a wall. Once framed
it won't change.   That is something!
And we'll take the papier-mâché
slap it on some boxes and fill them with candy
make use of this empty
make use; un-gone, re-something, unbroken.
I will weaponize mania
if it means I can time the joy
to coincide with my observed visitations.
My son will see me
happy   and won't know that I
am pretending to win the fight.
He has to know
that he is meant
to live even if

the cursed feet
visit him

:______________________
____
____

It won’t matter that my children are ghosts.
And sometimes I feel alive enough to—
sometimes I look at the sun and I do not flinch
sometimes I can reach out and grab it
turn the warmth around in my palm
feel the remnants of nuclear fusion
that braved the cold and the void
for millions of miles
just to shake my hand—

I am not whole.
But there’s enough of me
to try the daily work
of unbreaking.
And that is something.

Lyric

In the soft darkness
illuminated only by the twinkling

of Wi-Fi modem lights,
my steps on old, thin carpet—

somewhat muffled—
carrying you, Lyric, half-asleep,

bottle in one hand,
and the other—an outstretched arm,

fingers tickling loose
the surrounding air, a reaching

as to stretch—please
not yet. I lower my face into your hand.

You grab my nose,
a quick tug at tufts of unkempt hair

a finger sneaks
its way around my lip and

I'm fish-hooked.
The features of my face confirmed,

you drift,
though you are safe, you want

to know
who holds you, as do I.

I use my eyes
to commemorate your face

as it is now
to nuzzle you with mine.

If not for just
a couple more months

with you
as you are without prospect

of what you can be
just the aspect of sleep here

in my arms, shielded still
before having to claim agency over your soul.

Before the dice roll,
the genetic gamble of what you might become.

Just a little while longer.
Right now, I'm fine. But I will become worse and worse.

And the lines will uncouple.

The Custodian II

I am the devil that mops up after God
I am the mop   I am
The devil   The God
The devil after God
After God, the devil will mop me up
The mop will
Devil me

All of it will take place after God
After God does what?   Just after
Aftermath, aftershock?   Just after
The hourglass broken on the floor
Sand everywhere   It's just time but inside out
Grab the mop   Don the gloves
It's just my skin but inside out

Pick the glass   Out of my hands
Throw it in the trash
It's just my mop but inside out
It's just inside out   It's just
My insides
But out
Me mopped up but
My insides
Will out me
To the devil
It's just God but inside out

Last One to Die: Please Turn Out the Lights
For *Children of Men*

I'm all eyes and ears and it's all these people trapped in the crumbling this, they lived while the plot makes its murderous intrusion while they are the battleground, giving the earth to displace with explosions, the beams to shake, the joists to splinter and flesh—screams so loud that I can't help but stop to film them bleed while the plot keeps running that way—I'm only omniscience not omnipotence—there's so many bodies, I can't capture them all, so only the ones that still struggle, that agonize against the shaking ground that I can't cut, can't look away or my audience would forget them, forgot plot fodder has a voice, that war-torn has a face and many of them—I want to linger on these images that don't matter or rather they do because I noticed them—ethnography without words

Break the Rules

The walls call me weak when I
eat our sandwiches without crust.
The walls know I'll end up with dementia with,
and without: squeezed into an old folks' home,
debeaked and clipped wings.
I am, after all, no more a spring—after
all, these walls watch me
pick my nose, I'm flaring—scrounge up my scalp and collect it
under my fingernails, there's rules
boredom shows the world I care, I care
under my fingernails, one quick sabbatical around
the sun turns into lifelong hiatus.
If the walls would stop bickering, I'd talk more,
more for the river, they hope I'm becoming a river
oozing piss and shit into a very sad bag. Stop talking rancor already
and I'll take that hiatus from the outside world,
I'll make a sabbatical of the rules of the outside world—
spend an eon mashed between your white walls
chest tight and elbows raw against—
and my teeth squelch, they aren't real anymore.
They itch nonetheless for the garage sale down the street:
a hot zone for hand-me-down
death. I'm confessed by a sickness
onto rice cakes, onto refried beans, onto fireball summer, onto—
please, in time they might let me
mow the lawn. I didn't make the bet, please, the fractal grass is so long.
I'm corned by the sound
the VCR makes when it accepts another tape,
the equivalent of popping the next zit on my kneecap and
painting the walls the third time this week,
keep them quiet with a thick coat
of bleach so I can just—for a moment,
just—I wait here to leave, for the time strangle to gum me—

or a wholesome erosion into osteoporosis.
Waiting is yearning for death by formaldehyde, asbestos
drooling on my shirt, the one I didn't
eat yet. I'm a yellow tint episode, biting the ground right about now.
I'm as giving as a quarrel, boldly, whisky brands
line my bookshelf, howl of the forlorn squirrel
how many times the wheeling has already turned
and there's a want to explore the regret and blood moon
and the red beam guidance rips clouds to belief and requiem
and fret and the view from my second-story window
is a graveyard with waving murdered children.
I have to get out of this house, COVID be damned.
Hair has been jiving with my bed for several days,
suckle on the wall, and the micro feats earned each moment
I'm kept in here to confirm an execution
with concessions: my other shirt.

No, I'm breaking
the walls, I'm not
eating another shirt,
I'm running outside
and bursting into speckled light,
sheets of rain
billow around giving air
shape—I walk down the middle
of the street
because there's no cars on the road
and it's mine now.

Antagonize

No I want to be
eaten alive, that way I know
what's killing me.
I'm tired
of fighting intangible opponents.
I've been
carrying
weights until I pass
out, so I can
get a few good
punches in, make death
earn its meal, make death remember I broke
its nose I'm no protagonist
I'm the villain.
I'm not going to win
but it's going to remember me—
I will leave
a living stain which death must carry around.
When it comes to collect I will antagonize.
I'm going to tape a boning knife
to my hand, if I go
I'm going to die with the blade in my fist.
I can't fight this illness
but it's sure as hell going to fight me.
When it comes to devour,
I hope my skin is nothing
but gristle,
and that my bones break
its goddamned teeth.

Haunt

I convinced myself that when I grabbed the door handle and it refused to let me leave, that *I* was haunted. Not the house. From touching the cold metal, from that keyhole, I convinced myself I could see every time I left that house. I could see the last time I had to leave before I hurt myself or someone else. The only effective form of medication was to reduce environmental stressors, which were amplifying the symptoms. The anger and frustration of my household in Portland caused the symptoms, not the house. I hallucinated seeing the walls move, seeing little black spiders crawl out of the faces of people I thought were angry at me, hearing voices and all manners of sounds I cannot name. I would go from periodic bursts of mania where I believed I could see the future and the past, wouldn't sleep, wouldn't eat, wouldn't shower, or brush my teeth, followed by depression and inability to leave my bed. I was a nightmare to live with. I was no longer capable of being a good father, stepfather, or a good partner. When your reality is malleable, it is incredibly easy to convince yourself and to be convinced: I am not merely haunted, I will also be haunting. Of this, I was absolutely certain. No matter how hard I tried to resist, no matter how much I wanted to keep things together for the sake of the family, I was breaking. And if I did not leave, I would haunt.

Walking Away

I just have to know
It is 7:47 p.m.
Driving east across the remains of Lake Bonneville
Toward Salt Lake City into an indigo night
This world is a salt flat
The sun reminds me that it is setting
By peeking at my eyes through the rearview mirror
In the basin of
A ghost of
A lake
The horizon is wider than I have ever seen
It is called a flat
But I can see where the earth curves away
Right before it turns into mountains
The colors change from catacomb bone
To something I'm struggling to name
I just have to know
Spectrum of sunset cradled by
Jagged peaks on all sides
I'm in a coffin made for a titan
Perhaps its flatness
Is because Atlas dropped the sky
Since the sanctified rarity of rain
Has been here
The moisture-laden clouds are the floor
There is a thin film of water on portions of the flat
Acting as a perfect mirror
And I cry like I've never cried since
For all the colors I can't name
This is their moment
I just have to know
A paleolake is real again
This world is no longer

The valley of dry bones
I've misnamed
The massive coffin
I just have to know
It's a baptismal font

****

But blood spikes and strains against the walls of my veins
Sometimes we're plumbers
Fighting water hammer
I just have to know
It's a law of motion
Hydraulic shock simply is
With force, vacate the tear ducts
Entropy simply is
Why fight it
I have been forced
My psychologist and psychiatrist in agreement
I have to leave
I am a danger to myself and everyone around me
Because when the various meds don't work
Or are too expensive without benefits
It becomes stress
Because when you have to get your Master's
And teach during a pandemic
When you've never taught before
While dressed like a clown
It becomes stress
Because when you have to work three jobs
Just to afford a haunted house
It becomes stress
Because when you are one thousand miles away
From your closest friend or family member
And your partner hates that you exist

But refuses to let you leave
Because you are trying to rearrange your brain
I just have to know
Because you are not allowed
To leave the house
To take a shower
To watch TV
To work as much as you need to
I just have to know
Because you are trying to raise five children
It becomes stress
When you have schizoaffective disorder
And when you are stressed
With schizoaffective disorder
I can hear the march of spiders

****

7:50 p.m. and
It is hard to appreciate the colors of the sunset
When I can see the future of each tear
And I become delusion all over again
I've been wearing the same clothes for four days
And been sleeping in my car
I hold the steering wheel like my infant son
The last time I nuzzled his nose
And he grabbed a handful of my eyelid
I would like to blame the disorder
For walking away
But that seems too convenient
And on I-80 East
I don't think I deserve convenience
In deserts like these
I have always pushed on by working harder
But working harder becomes stress

And stress becomes more symptoms
I just have to know
What I can blame
And why these mountains feel like they can stare
And why every driver
Of every car I pass
Glares at me
I don't want to be a victim
But I don't want to create any either
It's hard to believe myself
When every window on every skyscraper in Salt Lake City
Is a reflective eye watching me drive along
I don't want to be a victim
But I need to suffer for this

****

She tried to make me hold my son
So that I couldn't run out the door
She thought I wanted to be free
But she didn't hear them
She didn't hear the ghosts of the murdered children
And what they were asking me to do
They've been doing it in the corner
Creating shadows
For hours now
I just have to know
I hugged my son while the house melted
Though I saw spiders crawl out of his eyes
I hugged him still and they crawled onto me
But he wasn't crying
So I knew the spiders weren't real

****

It is 7:52 p.m.
And I am not being baptized by Spirit
But by grief
I just have to know
I am only driving into freedom
If freedom rhymes with isolation
Freedom means I haven't brushed my teeth in a week
Because there is no one close enough
To tell me my breath stinks
Freedom means DoorDash
Means counting the fast food brown paper bags
Jenga their way to the ceiling
Freedom means rehearsing every possible conversation at work
Because you realize ironically
This makes you sound less crazy
Freedom means always living alone
So the ghosts and I can take turns playing warden
I hold them inside me
And I won't let them leave
I need to suffer for this

****

I hugged him as long as longing could last
But the angles of the room got sharper
The corners became deeper-voiced pits
I set him on the couch
The smile never leaving his tiny face
His curly brown hair made the silliest halo
I can't remember which animal was on his onesie
But I would confess if I could
I just have to know
I told him I loved him
As I shut the door
I walked off the porch

And onto a sheet of paper
I am a statistic
And I cried like I never cried before

****

It is 7:55 p.m. and the sun is gone
And I just have to know
I just have to know
I just have to know
I just have to
I just
No
I’ll tell you it isn’t real

****

PART IV

ALL THE THINGS I THOUGHT I WOULD NEVER SEE AGAIN

Of this, I am convinced
I would have died if I stayed in Portland
But leaving my son behind
Killed me anyway

The Custodian III

The newborn eyes of fulcrum innocence
counting brands in trash cans
and to betray the unlabored would spell
pale and squalor, scuffed fresh white Nikes,
a most horrible internal demise
bewitching
the habitual man with an untidiness
of sanity
so revolting in aspect and grossly glorious in dramatic
irony. These eyes upon that basement in my heart with prying distilled in
the storm
surge   and aftermath of billowed froth flung wide,
these hurricane centers so deadly   on the ground and entirely
majestic when viewed from above brought cataclysm
a bouquet of Vlasic kosher dills. The hell
do you make of that? This is what
I mean when I babble
about the connotation
of insanity. Calling something schizophrenic
is no longer just a lazy metaphor.
I don't reckon, I'm not here
to reckon but I can't help pulsating—
barbiturates and Barbasol,
the vivid, the sensation of
chewing 5 Gum
and my nerves ooze out of my pores in long strings of grapevines and
sinew
electric touch dangled, no, circumambulated
my throat   when I trap
my pupils   behind
my lids   to avoid the inquisitive roaring
stillness in those convexities containing hues of the spring
grass, of sunken

ice, of dying
leaves, the liquid
amber glass
that creates its own unit
of measurement.
It's hard to track time when your reason for living
is gone   with the children   all it took—

The Voyage (to Epitaph)

I have thirty-six hours left to drive
On my way to see my brother
For the first time in years

In Portland, I had mental funerals
For all the people
I thought I would never see again:

I: Burial

I knead you into the ground (the loss) I feel
A vessel (between) compacted ash I now
Pour out (the sides of my fingers angry with chunks
Of bone) together with the lingering dirt

I carry your specks (under my untrimmed nails)
And hold you as long as longing can
Outlast (the distance, a contraction)
The fear to fear too far (But under the soil

Relative, near) in time, I will come to imagine
(The bardo) you endure in the pollen and spores
Released from the garden of gardens of rhythm
And rhyme (become) the dirt between the dirt

Carry (my brother) home, where you can make
Your thumbs more green and see more sea
For you (no more) will I eat (for you cannot) until
The sails of your boat paint a different sky with white

II: Brother in the Wind

I'm sorry
It must have been my anger—weeds
Grew over you instead of orchids—but
Dandelions
Fertilized
With your ash
Can still sail—pappi
Released
In a gust
Of August haste
Together can billow
Like sails
Painting the sky and ground with white—I still
Have hope part of you will make it to
The sea

III: Brother at the Bar

In an attempt
To put your arm around a girl's shoulder
You miss quite a bit
The elaborate rings on your hand
Now tangled in her hair
But your laugh is contagious
So she laughs too
And she's yours

I smile and shake my head
Only because I'm your big brother
And DD
I pretend to disapprove
But honestly
I am baffled
Every single time

IV: Me, If You Were to Die

Would then be
The last in Illinois

I feel like I owe it to you
To imitate your effects on the flat land
A legacy effort
Dividends for your behavior
I imagine, with you gone
Walmart would have to ban me instead

I would need to start making
Bi-weekly barbershop appointments
To preserve your style
And unfairly photogenic hair

How in the world
Am I supposed to read and like
four thousand comments on TikTok?
Where did you get the time?

I will never understand
How you could electrify
The atmosphere
At 3:00 a.m.
Just by walking into the door
With a smile   You defibrillate each slumped guest
          Right back to life

V: Right Back to Life

When you were eleven
And sleepwalking
You occasionally drifted

Into my room
At 3:00 a.m.
Turned on the Xbox
"Finish the fight"
That's what you said
I watched you
In some bardo between awareness and dreams
Turn into Master Chief
Let's just say
You were much better when fully awake
But you could respawn then
It didn't matter how bad you were
A rocket to the face, a shotgun to the chest
Like I said
Right back to life

VI: Every

Single Time

That people say we have the same smile
And ask if we are alike
I gently tell them the truth
No
Not at all
Not even close

But
Every single time
I gently tell myself
I wish

But
In some ways
We are alike
In the strangest ways

We have the Jones Pace
Uncomfortable in stillness
Walking always
We make the world move like a treadmill
When everyone else is sitting down
I'm shadowboxing
You're hitting fadeaway jumpers
We stomp, we trample
We always had black, fungus-laden bare feet
We punish the ground for being the ground

Every single time we have a family reunion
And if we are coming
They must double the amount of food
If it's just one of us
Triple
If we both come
And there will still be no leftovers
We clean the table every single time
Licking the plates, scraping the edges of casseroles
Jealously shooing away flies
Or children we know will waste the food
We make gluttony an art display
People marvel at the calories, the meat sweats
We, forces of nature
Consuming all life has to offer

VII: The Deep Sleep

I oversaw waking you up
But no one could take sleep from you
To combat your deep sleep:
I made a trumpet
I took your blankets
I opened the window

I dropped a dog on your face
A bowl of hot soup
Poured on your feet

Somehow
Still
You sleep

When I was trying to wake you up
I would have
Loved to see
The happenings
In your dreams

Trying to wake you up

VIII: By Taking your Doorknob

It was a last resort
Your door was locked
It was 7:00 a.m.
A good six hours
Before I could expect you awake
My keys
Were in
Your room
Your screwdriver
Was in
My hand
No amount of pounding on the door
Had ever managed to work before
So I took your doorknob
And tried to reach you
Through the splintered hole
This new portcullis

IX: Forecasting

I find it incredibly ironic
That when you
A child
Were terrified of storms
And now
An adult
Child
Chase them for a living
You pray for them
You pray for their severity
You pray the winds can de-shingle houses
Tree branches puncture roofs
Windows shattered when the hail comes
Remnants, islands of glass
On seas of carpet

And when you come to that household torn
Biggest cheese-eating smile in the world
Sniffing your way to cheddar
You have the paperwork
They have the insurance
Claim that money right into your pocket

I know all too well. Door to door is rough.

When the season was dry
You tell me with nervous laughter
Some other workers
Would go up on the roof
With a ball-peen hammer
And do their best to imitate grape-sized hail

X: Forward Out to Sea

It's not your fault
(But) I'm upset

You went (to Haystack Rock) without me
Though I'd been there a dozen times
I wanted to be the one to (show) you (the coast)
See (the look on) your stupid face
I (wanted to) run (at your side)
The first time (you saw the Pacific)

Me (if I was there) with you
Taking (your picture while) you (showed off)
Your bottle of Hennessy
(Actually) I think it was two
Two (bottles of Hennessy)
One for each hand

And we could break death
(Stop) we could hear (the music) again
We (could we) could be (the music again)
(I could) look like (the tide
It slaps) you in the face
Embrace it though you may, (the pain) it drags
You under again roll (roll bro) you under again?
Don't (worry) I'm not (moving my feet)
(My legs are) buried (in the sand)
I've got (you
It's) my job
Your picture on my ceiling (was with me) in Portland
I'm (with) you now (Now I'm with you)
I'm (not) holding (you back) I'm pushing (you forward)
Farther out (to sea) where the waves are (kaleidoscopes)
The clouds (misty) meet (Haystack) ocean teeth underbite

The first (bite
the jaws of sky) snap shut (when face) full of salt
We (tumble again) I (am with) you
Forward we go (we go) forward
Wonder at (broken) time like one's (watch)
Nothing wound (nothing ticks) still
To feel (this potency) ticks
Possibly in your hair
And all (these scenic) interruptions
Of (escaped) breath to fill
The horizon as (it takes) another hot bite
(This time) out of your eyes
Jellyfish (dandelions dance on the wayward) beneath
And (there's so much) riverbanks
Follow (the song of
Gravity) here and how you can awake
For a moment (after eating sea salt taffy) and how
(Cheap car) air (freshener) can
Clear your mind and how blood (blisters)
Can remind you (how your feet work)
That you need (new shoes) that you
And the rigors (of travel) surmounted
Belong (seeking) to (to catch a patch of) new sky
This is real
Sky I see with you (you and I) we see

Unused Wedding Vow

In the downpour forecast
The muddy future of the ground
Depicting how optimistic is the statement
            "I will"
You're all hands and knees
Tending to the earthy slop
Hoping these perennials will bloom again and again
You razz me, "Learn to smell the roses."
But all I can promise

I will find the motivation to put the garbage out

Through marginal victories
The preservation of "I will"
            Sacred
There's a smile buried deep in my face
When I see your "I will"

You're ill
And five foot five
Playing basketball
But you promised to play
            So you will

You're in a hospital bed
With a huge grin
Because the nurse acquiesced
And changed the channel to *Family Feud*

It took your hair
And you responded in kind
By making an outrageous Kentucky Derby hat
It looked like you dragged it through the garden

I know you plant these for me
That they will come back again and again
Whenever winter threatens to break me
Still, you goad me to laugh

Your life speaks, "Treasure the victories in the margins."
The quiet success no one sees
The only triumphs you have ever known

For this and more, I give you my "I will"

The enormous strength it takes to be happy
While losing every day
Waiting for one instant to cherish
All that is left

The Eulogy

Al and his sister are now both dead. We grew up on the same street together, went to the same schools together starting in kindergarten and through senior year of high school.

When I was in fifth grade, I wrote comic books where my classmates got to be the heroes and villains. Each of them had their own powers similar to their real characteristics.

In the comics, Colin, Al's cousin, was corrupted and systematically killed off all of the heroes. In the end, the remaining heroes sacrificed themselves to kill the villains. I don't know why I'm so drawn to stories of sacrifice.

And by the end of the fourteenth chapter of these comics, everyone ended up dying. All except for Al. Because I felt bad, even in fiction, killing off someone who had no penchant for evil, who cared for everyone so deeply. Even though there was no story left to tell, I made sure he lived just because death did not deserve him. I know that's not how the universe works, but when I wrote my universe, he lived.

It was unbearably ironic that he was the first person from my class to die, like my wish for him to live ultimately sealed his fate.

I was even given a warning before he died. It seemed like what I struggled with, he might have struggled with too. I was asked to reach out to Al to see if I could talk to him.

But I didn't feel like I had the right. I hadn't talked to him in years by this point, and for me to suddenly reappear in his life like Gandalf to give unhelpful advice felt unfair to him. He wouldn't see Gandalf, he would see Forrest. So I didn't, I left it undone, and a couple months later, he died. This is a eulogy to him and many others.

However, I also want to eulogize

the dead parts
of me, that died alongside
my friends and family
and the parts that died while writing their poems.

It's almost as if when the final draft is sent in, a part of me dies with them, closed off forever. Nothing more about that person, place, or time, or the emotions I felt can be altered in that poem. Writings I have compiled for decades, whole chunks of my memory and feelings are no longer mine. It's like finishing *Return of the King*, and because of its many definitive endings, you mourn for the world that was created and all the stories that now feel dead. They are not being developed, Amazon be damned, they left the hands of their creators, and are effectively dead. They are unalterable, unchanging, rigor mortis.

Though I feel this, the dead and those I've lost touch with still visit me in my dreams, with new stories to tell of great exploits having conquered all the things they couldn't in life. It's the main reason I look forward to sleep and why I am so upset when my body won't let me. Because I feel like if I can't fall asleep, it's because I've left something undone.

But I do get to hear and see them again. And when I wake in a fog, struggling so vigorously to recall what happened and why they were there, it's like they won't let me remember the details. They only let me know that they were there and,

I felt warm
for them
having been.
After all, they have to
keep the story
going. And if I don't
remember it, they can
keep telling the story.
They can alter it, bring in new people,

tell different tall tales.
And because they can
keep changing
their stories, they don't
come back to life
in my dreams
just to experience
resurrection in reverse
when I wake up.
They're still alive,
a living body of work
a love story that can keep going
without a definitive end.

Daily Work

Yorkville has changed since I was last here.
There's an Arby's now

****

There is a daily act of excavation
To be unmade and reborn
I am digging up the bodies
Of all the people I thought I would never see again
I am unsaying their eulogies
I am mourning in reverse

But first, I had to dig myself out of my own tomb
I thought I would die in Portland
And now I have to do the daily work
Convincing myself I am still living

My first stop is Montana
To see Clayton who was
One of my teammates that came to Portland
One of many friends banned
Numbers deleted
I had to track down his info
Using a U-Haul database
Before I left without notice
My manager there, one of the best I ever had,
Of customers would say
Always assume a misunderstanding
Never assume someone is being malicious
With my leg bouncing
Sweating profusely
Snow on the ground
I finally told Clayton why

I had to push him away
And asked if he would
Be okay with
Being friends again

Colorado Springs in a hotel
Tim lets me sleep here while he works
Though he's glad to see me
Family is hard to see
While he literally builds bridges
Hard hat, sunglasses, company
Phone, and disgruntled employees
I try not to think about
Running away

The long drives on this broken road trip
To unbrake relationships are
Agony as I am still
Experiencing psychosis
And medication withdrawal
Montana to Colorado to Texas
I am screaming at myself
All the way down to
Austin
Is remarkably similar to Portland
Here to watch Eric play piano
In a crowded urban bar
I am relearning that I like music
But the mass of people is too much
The quarters too tight, beer free-flowing
Overstimulation is now a considerably rational fear
So my feet carried me to sidewalks outdoors
And I wandered for an hour until Eric finished his set
I am doing my best to unsee
But the trash in the crooks of the street

The sharps discarded in the city sprawl brush
It is daily work to not
Cross the street to avoid a passerby

While couch surfing at Josiah's apartment in Wisconsin
I stood up too fast and passed out
The weight of my body collapsed
Waking in the wreckage of a smashed end table
I tried to unbrake it
He laughed it off and helped me carry it to the dumpster
It is daily work to forgive myself
For not being able to
Put everything back together

****

It's a brisket sandwich with mayo and BBQ
Fried onion straws and curly fries
Sticky slop on my fingers
Normally, I won't eat with my hands
I hate trying to off-scrub the messy scuzz
In the remains of mutilated meals
Relearning that I can taste, touch, savor
Is daily work

It's sweatshirt season in Midwest 'burbs
I know because I am sleeveless
And can more precisely feel the fabric
Of my mom's Blackhawks sweater
When she hugs me on the front stoop
Normally, I hate being touched
I hate breathing the same air
I hate sharing warmth
I hate that someone else's
Hair is now on my clothes

I hate that I have to rely on other people
Allowing myself to be hugged is daily work

Allowing myself to be swept away
By something as small as a screensaver
It's a still of a jagged caldera in front of a lake
The peaks look like the palm of my hand
If I was laying down and looking at my flattened wrist
The muscle and tissue creating a ridge in the foreground
My fingers creating the peaks in the back
How massive must these mountains be
To make the lake look so small
And still, how large the clouds behind the mountains
And still, the sun, which isn't even in frame
Is so large that its light influences a picture
Pointing in the opposite direction
All of this size and beauty contained
On my small computer screen
Rather than answer emails
I stare at the photo for an hour
Because I am still trying
To find the name of the mountains
So to memory I must commit
This too, is daily work

Adobe Deli

As I was eating my pulled pork, brisket, and ribs, I became acutely aware of all the taxidermy animals and their glass eyes watching me savor what could have been their friends.

"More water, sir?"

"Yes, please." I was starting to sweat, and it wasn't because the food was spicy. Despite the numerous claims of the Adobe Deli in New Mexico being haunted, I didn't experience anything supernatural. Just unnatural, such as looking a mallard in the eye while eating the orange duck. There was not a square foot of open wall in the place, but for the first time, I didn't see or hear any ghosts. All the heads on the walls made the place feel like the walls could come down at any moment. The Adobe Deli didn't just house uncomfortable taxidermy animals, it was practically a warehouse of artifacts from countries and ages long past.

Some places are not haunted by ghosts but by stories, stories lost to history, stories I can only guess at, but nevertheless cling like skin to its fur —a texture I will never touch. This was a collection of secret histories disguised as a steakhouse.

There were animals in there so old the skin was peeling off the frame, so loose that the marble eyes fell out and bounced on the dark wood floors. Rumor has it these older ones were made by a man who murdered his wife, but that doesn't interest me. I am not haunted by the rumors and hearsay, I am haunted by what will forever be unknown; I am someone who just has to know.

Before leaving the Adobe Deli, I walked around the rooms to study each of the artifacts to see if I could sense a connection: a delusional transcendental moment where I intimately knew who used the old oven in the lounge, what the deer on the wall's last meal was before being shot, how many times these vinyl records were played in someone's house during the Blitz. I couldn't. Though that should be cause for celebration, I am someone who just has to know. I want to know why there are so many wooden ox yokes and what life is like to bear one. I want to imagine myself as part of the decor, that the Adobe Deli has collected me as well. And if my job is to haunt for the sake of ambiance, let me hint at stories untold. There are truth lacerations in the foundation. Should I put in the effort to hide a part of me? It's not who I am, but it is an unchanging reality. How much cracked load-bearing walls, flawed cornerstones, and rotting wood can I accumulate? How many animal masks can I hang on the walls before they all come down? Rather than wait for the collapse, I will finally unlock the door.

Thanksgiving for the POMC

I want to imagine
The ghost children
I want to give them credit
After all, two giant trees fell
In our yard on Duane Street
Both of them missed the house
By inches, preferring instead
To crush my neighbor's truck
If I am forced to accept the haunting
As a potential reality
I will choose to think the children
Of the POMC memorial
Were not malicious
Just misunderstood
And incredibly lonely
Because the house never felt
Antagonistic though it did
Trap and hold, things
Needed to be held on to
A blanket, a teddy
Here too, a eulogy
To the murdered children
For always meeting me halfway

****

Despite the greenery
the building forest of sound
the difference between rustling and crinkling
leaves on the branch   still   versus leaves tread upon.

Crickets and frogs anathemizing
the Pacific Northwest.

Despite

your former love
for the smell of prairie lavender
rows of color beyond the forest clearing
childhood held delicately like a moth
a flashlight used to see through its wings—

running with your cousins
        to the nearest park
            after the adults
                fell into food sleep
                too much turkey.
                Too much.

It took one moment
for us
to never speak
of this place again—

            when running
and the downed branches you loved climbing
a stumbling block,
            when the rustling leaves
                crinkled under your bruised body—
                the leaves underneath you
                                                    were dragged by
your feet
                                                to the lavender field.

        Your hair collecting twigs and
            roly-polies
            your first friends
hiding inside their defense.

Whether it was a chemical imbalance
or the result
of hatred to the third and fourth generation,

that man still stabbed you thirty-nine times. A death sentence for two.

For me
to say   *I'm sorry—*
a greater emptiness
than this current silence.

Still   I want you to know
I'm here
and the sun is here
and the wind is here.
And I am not that man.

        As selfish as it may be
I need to know
you're not still being tortured, trapped
        in a curled, greying ball
punctured
                                                by your own limbs.
Too much.
I need to know   that finding you
in his hastily constructed mass grave
doesn't bind you
or me
here.

As I walk   circles
the blood-stained earth
with a priest sprinkling holy water
to set you free from the tangles of lavender,
I bite my tongue
hard   enough
that there are indents
your presence can fill,

that you may always be on my tongue
when freedom is yours again
and I can't find you here
but in the words and stories I tell—

that you tackled people when you hugged them;
your grandma said
she felt the sun's warmth:
your cheeks pressed against hers.

You blew the wind on wet dog noses
so they would be as excited as you.

And I am
so lucky
you loved nature
that when you wove
wisteria, daisies, lavender shoots
into your hair,
you grafted nature into my heart
and I find you
every time
I drive by a park.

I hope it is as easy
for you to find me
if you wanted to visit
just for a little bit
I promise
not to give you
a Midwestern goodbye:
a farewell
longer
than the Thanksgiving dinner we actually came for.

With so many leavings
here in the prairie
it's hard
not to make goodbye
the main event.

Counterpunch

As of 2022, the positive symptoms are gone. Positive meaning that they are in addition to who I am: hallucinations, disorganized cognitive functioning, catatonia.

The negative ones remain. Those that take away from me: reduced social skills, anhedonia, self-destructive behavior, mood disorders. My Apple watch measures the Jones Pace which I suspect will never leave. It tells me that I often will walk ten miles a day entirely inside my office. Just pacing back and forth and thinking.

But I found ways to counter the symptoms when they appear.

I became a teacher, and so I must constantly be expressing myself all day. This fights my tendency to isolate and not speak.

I find it funny that my usually flat affect and need to feel pain go hand in hand, or glove in glove, as I took up boxing. It's inexplicable, but I like being punched in the face. So now I am a very happy person. Because Nick, my boxing coach, is very good at punching me in the face.

Though there is no amount of push-ups
That can help me beat
An enemy no one can see
This violence
The world does to my body
And what I permit to be done
May I remember
It's a not a fight
It's a dance
Atop Mt. St. Helens or
Atop the peaks of the Torres del Paine
My new screensaver

Eternal Recurrence II

Or, if say, my plane goes down on the red-eye flight
and I have to relive the clicking
of the mouse and clacking keys for card information,
the drive to the airport that I left five hours
early for, because of traffic and O'Hare's tendency
to be crowded on the O'Holidays.
And I have to live through TSA
and pay fourteen dollars for a singular taco
and sitting in cramped rows while I pretend
to read but can't because
I am aware of the vast variety
of person noises from chewing
to mouth-breathing to foot tapping to
back cracks to thumbs hitting a keypad,
stomachs reacting to first-time Cinnabon
and then we're walking and boarding
and heaving luggage then waiting
then waiting some more
crammed between strangers and waiting
to the point that you can almost clock
the rate at which your hair grows.
If I have to relive this death and all of that
you can bet my favorite part
will be the free fall
I will choose to slow down the moment
when I pull out a picture of my son
and the people next to me do the same
and suddenly we're not strangers anymore.
I'm not merely a disorder.
We're just people fighting death
against time and space to see
their families on Christmas.

Love in the Ring

Shoes laced with precision, to constrict
        The pressure, a reminder that you should not feel feet
But be shoe, to forget one has limbs
        That can ache, that can bruise
Forgetting that there is an insatiable
        Itch buried deep in a heavily calloused footpad
That you won't be able to scratch anyway
        Especially not now as the bell rings and
The fists swing and the sweat bursts
        Off gloves like moisture fireworks
The hands too, buried in twelve ounces of leather
        And some kind of protective stuffing
Are not meant to be hands, but hammers
        Forget you have fingers or hairy knuckles
All you have is a pair of WWI trench clubs
        Ready to maul and pummel to better
Position the reduction of phalanges
        The fist stitched shut for bludgeoning
Until the opponent decides, willingly or not
        There are diminishing returns to being punched in the face
But the real art is forgetting
        You have a face altogether
Since it isn't even recognizable at the moment
        It's an oval-shaped void behind gloves
It's transparent, it fluctuates
        Your face is akin to photons
Wave and particle, harder to hit
        Forget you have eyes, one swollen shut
And a cauliflowered ear, and a busted lip
        Forget you are trying to breathe
Through a dentist-approved horseshoe wedged
        In your mouth, erasure is the athlete's contribution
To art, obliviate consciousness and be force

There's no time to think anyway
You can't think about how your opponent has transferred
The warmth emitting from his face
To your glove, and that you have a phantom sensation
Of his warmth, his will and vigorous blood
Staining your hand, that his rib
Broke with such force the sound
Vibrated up your arm
Thinking is for before and after
At face-off and clumsy, fingerless hug
After the final ring, empathy is not
What it seems in this sport
Because there's something really wrong with both of you
Who enjoy pain waaaaaay too much
So much it could be considered clinical
And not just the pain but the forgetting
Of a body that can experience it
Transcendence of pain, a brutal gift
Offered to the panting, anthropomorphic shadow that is not
Human for the next twelve rounds, empathy
In boxing is respecting that your opponent wants
Everything you got, wants to wear a skin
Of agony and push through it
Yes, there is pain and in this pain
There is tremendous love for pain itself

This Is Not a Good Poem

It is a thesis. The schizophrenic spectrum is vast. Relatively, I am considered high functioning. Others have it much, much worse. However, we are much more like you than you think.
I have dreams. I want the best for everyone. I don't want to hurt people.

I just sometimes have dreams while still awake.

Confusion, discovery, denial, understanding, recovery.
All are vital parts of living with any lifelong illness.
Every person has an asterisk.

If I look at myself now and myself before the symptoms started in eighth grade, it's fascinating to ask myself the question, "What about me has changed?" Honestly, not that much. My brother and I still seek out Quiznos subs because Papa fueled our Baja chicken addiction. I had an uncompromising work ethic then, and I am the same way now. I probably work even harder to oppugn the things I'm dancing with.

And if I am forced to meaning make, my symptoms are a thermometer. I am often too gullible or naïve to sense danger.

Now I know
that hallucinations
are a stop sign
a warning to leave a situation for my own safety;

that my mood disorders
coincide with isolation
or conversely
with being overwhelmed
and I can adjust as need be;

that my OCD tendencies

are a Hegelian dialectic
to offset motivation issues;

that a moderate amount of self-hatred
and a weird love to endure physical pain
if acted upon productively
can give me the will to become a better person.
After all, if I don't dislike some aspect of myself
I will never be moved to change.

Because I still need to
be moved and moving
so that I occasionally must do battle with the little black spiders.

Like it's some epic childhood conquest to keep them off my windowsill. I can kill them now, and there's a certain chemical smell released from all of their bodies after I flatten them. I've been thinking that this smell reminds me of something, but I can't quite meet it yet. It's funny that this morbid process should provoke stirred memories whether pleasant—chlorine, it's chlorine but not exactly. It's a swimming pool, but dingy, mistreated, overused, and unkempt as I imagine my cousins never put new chemicals in the pool. And we were young too, so there were all kinds of things going into that pool. The color was always shimmering between the off-white of the pool floor, the blue reflection of the sky, some sort of just-visible green leafy mildew nonsense, and the unspeakably yellow. This pool housed treasured memories in a dirty, leaf-covered chemical stink. This is where I first learned to swim and swim against the whirlpool created by the violent gaggle of children running in circles. Pool noodle fights and—hey, you can't eat your corndog in the pool. And then, just as violently, Illinois would decide summer was over and lower the temperature from the sweltering and humid nineties down to the thirties and forties of early fall, sometimes overnight. And the dark blue tarp would stretch itself miraculously over our memories and contain our games for another year. I never saw it happen. It's a veiny navy with cerulean creased marks that haphazardly grid the tarp in a network of capillaries that remember how the tarp was folded, how it was stowed away for months, how it stretched and contorted in cycles. The spiders had a harder time getting into the pool then. I now know how to keep them away. They are not welcome here because they are strikingly not blue.

Now I know
that despite it all
this is not a death sentence.
Despite it all
I am not the spiders.
And even if I see them again,
spiders have an uncanny resemblance to asterisks;

and asterisks are just another inclusion in a long list of things yet to be understood.

You Cannot Look Away

It's a cliche, I know
But the chances of driving you home
And out the window color lingers
Despite how common the trope
And though punctuation is still rare
In the forecast, I see escape
Via arcs of chromaticity

And the spray and the lines
Smote across the sky in the parallel
Boundaries that were never really there
But they, and this is where we get technical,
Refracted all at once, the millions
The particles and their dust addendum
Projection and shimmer held in a breath

A forecast of pure in-realism
And the treason felt by the sun's rays
As atmosphere clashes back against ultraviolet
Spectacle for us onlookers and oops
Fender benders, not watching the road
Since previously unobserved
But I did not fantasize about death

In this collision, I dream
Verdant skeletons regrow in this strange
Blend of light preventing anthropomorphic shadows from
Our skin caught in the moment
Between rain and an acute 42 degrees
Of photon blasts ransacking the freshly formed
Renewed retinas, and all

The things that give pause
How dare we even think of insurance
During these slight moments of sky melt
With firmament cataract unclouded, you
Say to me, just imagine
Imagine how big a rainbow must be
To something that can see the full spectrum of light

ACKNOWLEDGMENTS

"Antagonize" originally published as "Antagonise" (Aussie spelling) first appeared in *Antithesis* Volume 31. Additionally, the poems "Everything is Fine" and "Saturn Devouring His Son" were first published in *Poems that Express Nemesis* by Poet's Choice.

The quoted section in the poem "I Went Walking" is paraphrasing James Stuart Blackie's translation of Goethe's *Faust*.

I would like to thank all of my friends who continue to put up with my shenanigans. Notably, I would like to thank Eric Baker of Wrongbird and Luke Underhill of Playing with Fireworks for making great music and talking all kinds of art; Josiah Hahn and the rest of the Hahn family for housing me for several months when I left Portland; Clayton Birkes, Erik Franklin (who gave me the title "Life Is Made Possible by the Lies we Tell Ourselves"), Austin Springsteen, Tom Olivieri, Gibson Odderstol, and Zach Gettes for helping me turn Coe College into a Rube Goldberg machine of continuous mischief; Kevin and Kami Beardsley for making childhood an unrivaled period of joy; and Nick Maldonado for teaching me how to box and retake my life.

For my former professors, I would like to thank Meira Kensky, Geoff Chaplin, and Chris Hatchell for shaping how I see and interact with the world and for being damn good people; Nick Twemlow for converting me to poetry and showing just how many writing tools I hadn't used yet; John Beer and Michele Glazer for being remarkably patient and knowledgeable even when I was losing it.

From my family, I would like to thank Connor Jones for making life a party and for letting me mooch off him for his friends; Lyric Allen for being unapologetically brimming with wonder and joy; Cymber Jorgensen for always being a great mother even when I didn't want it; Paul Jones for being wiser than he probably believes; Joanne Buchner for framing my first check from a poetry prize; Tim and Lisa Meyer for being the other best part of my childhood; Brad and Maria Buchner for continuously feeding me cheesecake and letting me hang out with their dogs; and all of dad's siblings, Marie, David, and Mike for holding the family together with hilarious holiday gatherings.

For my Toyota Camry who has gotten me across the country more times than I can count over the past twelve years. May you keep moving forward.

Many names have been altered if they are associated with sensitive issues. Some presences are still very much connected with this book even if they only appear as pronouns. It is irresponsible of me to include the real names of the dead or of people who suffered and suffered with/because of me.

ABOUT THE AUTHOR

Anton Jones is a professor and program lead of the English department at Concordia University Chicago. He teaches English and creative writing while assisting with the publication of the university's two literary magazines: *Motif* and *Caesura.* He attributes his love for writing to a decade spent composing silly poetry around a campfire with his best friends. You can connect with Anton on Instagram @atjones43.

www.ingramcontent.com/pod-product-compliance
Lightning Source LLC
Chambersburg PA
CBHW031526120626
46545CB00005B/2028
9781957430249